Prejudice and Literature

Prejudice and Literature

J. Mitchell Morse

Temple University Press
Philadelphia

Temple University Press, Philadelphia 19122
© by Temple University. All rights reserved
Published 1976
Printed in the United States of America
International Standard Book Number:
  0-87722-072-7
Library of Congress Catalog Card Number:
  76-20169

To Frances, Carolyn, Jon, Haesun, and Maria

Contents

Preface

When we take metaphors and abstractions literally, they become phantoms and haunt us. We are haunted by the Body Politic, the Heir to Culture, the Natural Man, the Unstable Woman, the Evil Intellectual, and other cheap phantoms.

This book is an effort to exorcise them by seeing them for what they are—words, words, words—and indicating the processes by which they have come to be taken for realities.

Acknowledgments

This book has grown in the
stimulating atmosphere of Temple University; I have
benefited by the conversation of many colleagues here,
and by the correspondence of others throughout the
country. My very special debts to Adaline Glasheen, the
Joycean, and to Maurice English are indicated by notes
to several chapters.

My wife, Frances, has listened to many versions of
each chapter, and has made me cut, add, cool down,
heat up, reorganize, make smoother and make rougher; I
have learned from experience that she is always right;
nevertheless, in one case I have disregarded what is
probably her better judgment. Our son, Jonathan, has
written me a number of letters with knowledgeable and
incisive comments, which have resulted in improvements
in many chapters; and our daughter, Carolyn, has
changed my view of life for the better in many ways that
are reflected in the pages that follow.

Chapter 1 was read at the annual business meeting of
the College Section of the National Council of Teachers

of English, November 23, 1973, and was published in
College English, February 1974. Chapter 10 was also
published in *College English,* April 1976. For permission
to reprint these chapters I thank the copyright holder,
the NCTE.

For permission to quote other copyrighted materials, I
thank the following:

The Beacon Press and James Baldwin for James
Baldwin's "Stranger in the Village," in *Notes of a Native
Son,* copyright 1955 by James Baldwin.

The Bollingen Foundation for François Valéry's
preface to *History and Politics,* in *The Collected Works of Paul
Valéry,* trans. Denise Folliot and Jackson Matthews,
copyright 1962 by the Bollingen Foundation.

Delacorte Press for Allen Tate, ed., *T. S. Eliot: The
Man and His Work,* copyright 1966 by Delacorte Press.

Dodd, Mead for Winston Churchill, *A History of the
English Speaking Peoples,* 1956–58, copyright by Dodd,
Mead.

Doubleday & Co. for Francis Golffing, trans.,
Nietzsche, *The Genealogy of Morals,* Doubleday Anchor
Books, copyright 1956 by Doubleday & Co.

Faber & Faber for Ezra Pound, *Polite Essays,* copyright
1937 by Faber & Faber.

Farrar, Straus & Giroux and Roger Kojecky for Roger
Kojecky, *T. S. Eliot's Social Criticism,* copyright 1971 by
Roger Kojecky.

Gallimard for Valery Larbaud, *Oeuvres,* Editions de la
Pléïade, copyright 1958 by Gallimard.

Grove Press for Samuel Beckett, *Murphy,* copyright
1958 by Grove Press, and for *The Autobiography of Malcolm
X,* copyright 1966 by Grove Press.

Harcourt, Brace & Co. for T. S. Eliot, *The Idea of a
Christian Society and Notes towards the Definition of Culture,*
copyright 1940 and 1949 respectively by Harcourt, Brace
& Co.

Harcourt, Brace, Jovanovich, for *T. S. Eliot, The Waste
Land, Facsimile and Transcript,* ed. Valerie Eliot, copyright
1971 by Harcourt, Brace, Jovanovich.

Harcourt, Brace & World for *Letters of Ezra Pound 1907–1941,* ed. D. D. Paige, copyright 1950 by Harcourt, Brace & World; and for *The Collected Essays, Journalism and Letters of George Orwell,* ed. Sonia Orwell and Ian Angus, copyright 1968 by Sonia Brownell Orwell.

Alfred A. Knopf for D. H. Lawrence, *The Plumed Serpent,* copyright 1955 by Alfred A. Knopf.

The Macmillan Co. for Bernard Bergonzi, *T. S. Eliot,* copyright 1972 by The Macmillan Co.

McGraw-Hill for Alfred Appel, Jr., ed., Vladimir Nabokov, *The Annotated Lolita,* copyright 1970 by McGraw-Hill.

New Directions for *Literary Essays of Ezra Pound,* ed. T. S. Eliot, copyright 1968 by New Directions; and for *The Cantos of Ezra Pound,* copyright 1970 by New Directions.

New York University Press for J. Mitchell Morse, *The Sympathetic Alien,* copyright 1959 by the New York University Press.

Pantheon Books and Noel Stock for *The Life of Ezra Pound,* copyright 1970 by Noel Stock.

G. P. Putnam's Sons for Vladimir Nabokov, *Speak, Memory,* copyright 1966 by G. P. Putnam's Sons.

Random House for James Joyce, *Ulysses,* copyright 1966 by Random House.

Schocken Books for Jean-Paul Sartre, *Anti-Semite and Jew,* trans. George J. Becker, copyright 1968 by Schocken Books.

Viking Press for *The Collected Poems of D. H. Lawrence,* copyright 1929 by Jonathan Cape and Harrison Smith, Inc.; for *The Letters of D. H. Lawrence,* copyright 1932 by the Estate of D. H. Lawrence; and for *Letters of James Joyce,* ed. Stuart Gilbert, copyright 1957 by the Viking Press.

Yale University Press for James Hall Pitman, trans., *The Riddles of Aldhelm,* copyright 1925 by the Yale University Press.

Prejudice and Literature

1

Blood, Soil, and Culture

In my first year of teaching English my freshmen wrote one of their themes in response to a story entitled "The Petrified Giant," which had to do with a large rock formation so named and its psychological effects on the people who lived near it. One girl wrote, "This story doesn't make sense because a giant is bigger and stronger than anybody so why should he be petrified." When we went over her paper in my office I asked her, "What does 'petrified' mean?" " 'Scared,' " she said. "You know—petrified. Like when you're petrified." That was my first experience of a person who knew the metaphorical meaning of a word but not the literal meaning.

Some fifteen years went by before I met another—this one a Ph.D. candidate in English. In a seminar on *Finnegans Wake* we were discussing a passage in which Humphrey Chimpden Earwicker dreams that he is accused of many sexual abnormalities, including bestiality with a dog, a hen, a fish and a clothes horse. In honest puzzlement a student asked, "What's so abnormal

about having sexual relations with a clothes horse?"
"Well, what is a clothes horse?" I asked. "A beautiful
woman," he said. "One that makes clothes look good."

And recently, in an advanced writing class, a lovely
lissome virginal clothes horse majoring in English wrote,
"I suffered a great deal in my childhood because my
older brother was a bastard." The rest of the paragraph
made it clear that she had suffered because her brother
had taken pleasure in knocking her down, breaking her
toys, etc. When I told her that she should have used

another word or phrase, because the use of "bastard" in
that context involved an unintended ambiguity and was
momentarily misleading, I discovered that she didn't
know its literal meaning.

This is a rather rare disorder of the vocabulary; but it
is not limited to college students. During a Senate
debate in 1972 as to whether the United States should
honor its commitment as a member of the United
Nations not to buy chrome from Rhodesia so long as
that country violated the U.N. Charter of Human Rights
by denying civil rights to blacks, Senator Robert C. Byrd
of West Virginia, a politician since 1946, who one would
think had learned somewhere along the way the literal
meanings of the words "majority" and "minority,"
denied that the Rhodesian government, representing
250,000 whites, discriminated against "minorities"—
meaning the 4,750,000 blacks.

The opposite disorder, that of taking a metaphor
literally, is much more common and does much more
harm. The principal of a high school where students and
teachers are mugged in the halls offers parents the
consoling thought that the school is suffering "growing
pains." If that statement means anything, it means that
muggings in the halls are nothing to worry about, that in
due course they will cease as unaccountably as they
began, and that meanwhile nothing can be done about
them. It is totally irresponsible. And a number of
historians have said that Sir Winston Churchill wasted

thousands of lives by insisting that the first Allied offensive of World War II be aimed at "the soft underbelly of Europe"—i.e., at mountainous Italy rather than at flat Normandy—a metaphor that many believe reflected a vulgar racial prejudice, but in any case one that showed him thinking of Europe as a man or an animal rather than as a body of land.

To take a literal term or statement metaphorically is so rare that it startles, shocks or amuses us, and so does little harm; but we take metaphors literally so often that we don't realize that we are doing it—and therein lies great danger. Consider, for example, the seemingly innocuous metaphor "our cultural heritage."

The notion that there is a cultural "heritage"—a body of arts, sciences, letters, customs, manners and amenities that some people by virtue of their race or nation "inherit" and others don't—is a metaphor that ruins millions of people's lives, but it is accepted even by some of those whose lives it ruins. James Baldwin has expressed this acceptance perfectly in "Stranger in the Village": the citizens of a Swiss village where he spent two summers, despite their friendliness to him, despite the fact that they had less knowledge of the European arts and sciences than he, nevertheless regarded him, "quite rightly," he says, "not only as a stranger in their village but as a suspect latecomer, bearing no credentials, to everything they have—however unconsciously—inherited."

For this village is the West, he says, and would be even if it were more isolated and less developed; and these villagers "have made the modern world, in effect, even if they don't know it. The most illiterate among them is related, in a way that I am not, to Dante, Shakespeare, Michelangelo, Aeschylus, Da Vinci, Rembrandt, and Racine; the cathedral at Chartres says something to them which it cannot say to me, as indeed would New York's Empire State Building, should anyone here ever see it."

Here a victim of racism has taken a racist metaphor literally, and so unconsciously encouraged its currency. For of course that village is not the West; it is only an isolated village; no creative Western idea is known to its inhabitants, but only a few superstitions; they have not made the modern world, for they have not made anything—what does the phrase "in effect" mean? And they are not related in any way to any work of art that they have not experienced, for such relations are personal and depend entirely on personal experience. If Baldwin has read *Emile* he has established a relationship with Rousseau; if those Swiss villagers have read nothing of Rousseau's they have established no relationship with him, and the fact that he was Swiss does not constitute one for them. We don't acquire a relationship with works of art in the same way that we acquire our citizenship, merely by being born in one place rather than another or of one race rather than another; relationship with a work of art or a body of art is an attainment, an achievement, not a gift of nature or custom. No race or nation has an exclusive proprietary right, or an exclusive biological ability, to enjoy the products of its culture. Strictly speaking, no race or nation has a culture of arts and letters; a culture of that kind lives and has its being only in those individuals who have become acquainted with it.

But exclusive proprietary rights to it, and an exclusive racial ability to enjoy it, are always claimed by racists— that is, by those racists who are aware of it at all. Sartre, in *Anti-Semite and Jew,* reports that a classmate of his, who failed the *agrégation,* resented the fact that a Jew had passed, saying, "You can't make me believe that that fellow, whose father came from Cracow or Lemberg, understood a poem by Ronsard or an eclogue by Virgil better than I." That such an attitude was not merely that of a student who had flunked his exams Sartre indicated by paraphrasing Maurras to the effect that no Jew could possibly understand Racine, because such understanding is a matter not of literary knowledge or sensitivity but of French blood and soil: something every "true Frenchman" is born with and no Jew can acquire.

But Jean Chapelain, a "true Frenchman" if ever anyone was, insisted that his flatulent epic *La Pucelle, ou La France Delivrée* was great because it observed all the rules of epic composition; and Richelieu, a "true Frenchman" if ever anyone was—one moreover who liked to think of himself as a patron of literature—rated Chapelain above all other writers, and on his advice gave purses, pensions, estates, monopolies and sinecures to many mere pedants and poetasters now forgotten, but none to Corneille, whose *Le Cid* in fact he suppressed, alleging literary inadequacy and the necessity of maintaining minimum standards in the theater. The members of the French Academy, "true Frenchmen" all and guided by Chapelain, concurred unanimously in the unfavorable judgment Richelieu wanted.

Montaigne, on the other hand, being half Jewish, was presumably no more a "true Frenchman" and no more capable of writing good French prose than Proust; Heine was notoriously not a "true German" and therefore was presumably not endowed with a feeling for German verse—during the Nazi period, let us recall, German anthologists either omitted Heine's poems or attributed them to "Anonymous"; Pushkin, a black man and therefore not a "true Russian," was presumably incapable of understanding, to say nothing of writing, Russian poetry; and since Terence, an African who went to Rome as a slave, was not a "true Roman," his plays— the wittiest, most polished of Roman comedies—have been attributed to Scipio the Younger for reasons of the same kind as those for which the plays of Shakespeare have been attributed to the Earl of Oxford. Into such irresponsibilities does the metaphor of a cultural birthright lead us.

Closely related to the metaphor of a cultural birthright or heritage is the metaphor of a social heritage or birthright or fate. Few would now maintain out loud and in public the old doctrine that hereditary social classes are divinely ordained and that the good life consists in doing our duty in the station in which it pleased God to place us at birth; in the Western world the fact of social mobility has long since pushed that idea into the dim background and replaced it in the forefront of our minds with a paradox: the idea that since we are individually free to rise or fall to our natural social level, the lower levels are genetically inferior to the upper levels: so that hereditary classes, which we used to think were ordained by God, we now think are inherent in biology. This is a change of metaphor that disguises a persistence of belief.

To be sure, the metaphor that we inherit our natural social status as we inherit the color of our eyes, hair or skin is not *officially* accepted, as the metaphor of divine ordination was; our whole system of public education is evidence that we recognize the fact of unequal opportunities—it is an official effort to reduce as much as possible the unfair advantages and disadvantages with which children born in different neighborhoods enter the competition. But, as we all know, for many reasons, not the least of which is the personal indifference or hostility of many officials to the official doctrine, the schools are not as effective as they should be in overcoming the inequalities of nurture. To maintain "neighborhood schools" is to institutionalize such inequalities: it is to insist, officially, not only that class differences are more important than individual differences, but also, in effect, that there are no individual differences. (Here, the term "in effect" means just what it says.)

Let us consider the effects of unequal nurture on two unmistakably gifted writers of our own day. William James tells us that extreme, exaggerated and abnormal cases help us to understand normal life because they isolate and illuminate its constituent factors, enabling us "to inspect them unmasked by their more usual surroundings." Let us consider, therefore, on the one hand the extreme case of Vladimir Nabokov, and on the other hand the extreme case of Malcolm X.

When Nabokov's biographer Alfred Appel, Jr., asked him what he had read as a boy, he replied: "Between the ages of ten and fifteen in St. Petersburg, I must have read more fiction and poetry—English, Russian, and French—than in any other five-year period of my life. I relished especially the works of Wells, Poe, Browning, Keats, Flaubert, Verlaine, Rimbaud, Chekhov, Tolstoy, and Alexander Blok. On another level, my heroes were the Scarlet Pimpernel, Phileas Fogg, and Sherlock Holmes. In other words, I was a perfectly normal trilingual child in a family with a large library" (Introduction to *The Annotated Lolita* [New York: McGraw-Hill, 1970], pp. xliii-xliv).

A perfectly normal three-headed child! How many perfectly normal children live in families with large libraries, to say nothing of full-time tutors and governesses who are native speakers of the languages they impart? Of course those riches (and the sense of security, well-being, warmth, love and unending discovery he gratefully remembers in the early chapters of *Speak, Memory*) didn't make Nabokov the genius he is —they didn't make any of the four other children in that home a genius—but certainly they stimulated his growth and eased his development and made it possible for his work to take the evidently congenial forms it did take. Given Nabokov's obviously superior native intelligence, it is quite possible that he would have written *something* even if he had not grown up under such superior conditions; but it is inconceivable that such complex jewels as *Lolita, Pnin* and *Pale Fire* could have been made by a monolingual man trained not in literature but in bookkeeping; and all the evidence indicates that an illiterate man, however great his native intelligence, could have written nothing. It is embarrassing to point out something so obvious, but alas—as we shall see—it is necessary.

Nabokov's ancestors on both sides had been aristocrats of large fortune for six centuries, and among the many generals and high public officials had been a few minor poets, some pretty good musicians, and several scholars of some distinction, including a woman M.D. in the nineteenth century who wrote on psychiatry, anthropology and social welfare. But no genius is to be accounted for altogether in genetic terms; some opportunity to develop is essential. For a writer, e.g.— and I emphasize this seemingly obvious fact because the highly intelligent Francis Galton couldn't see it, and many more or less intelligent people still can't see it— for a writer, literacy is essential; but literacy has been denied to most people in most places throughout most of literate human history. Virgil was the son of an illiterate farm hand who had married the farmer's daughter and inherited the farm and taken care to give his son a literary and philosophical as well as agricultural education; Horace was the son of a slave who had bought his freedom and become a farmer and taken care to give his son a literary and philosophical education; both these poets in their youth were permitted to lead lives of studious leisure—rare good fortune for boys born in their class. Bossuet, the supreme master of French classic eloquence, came of a peasant family which because of its royalist loyalist fervor during the wars of religion had been enabled by the church and the crown to rise to the status of provincial magistrates; Chekhov, the grandson of an illiterate serf who had bought his family's freedom, was sent to medical school by his father; and even Jean Genet, with all his unspeakable misfortunes, was taught to read and write in childhood. J. M. Robertson, in "The Economics of Genius" (which can be found in V. F. Calverton's anthology *The Making of Society* [New York: Modern Library, 1937], pp. 624–55), observes that of 110 good European writers who lived during the six hundred years from 1265 to 1865, only two—Bunyan and Burns—were the sons of poor men, and both of these had exceptional opportunities. He might have added Carlyle.

If it be argued that this fact indicates some genetic superiority in the parents or earlier antecedents, it must also be observed that they too, in every case, benefited from exceptional opportunities. Robertson takes issue on theoretical grounds with the hereditarian Francis Galton's theory that genius always succeeds regardless of circumstances and that no improvement of the circumstances of life would increase the amount of genius available to society—that the far greater availability of education in America, for example, has not produced a proportionately greater amount of first-class intellectual work, and that if the lack of elementary schooling in England were remedied there would be no noticeable increase in such work there. But Robertson accepts as fact Galton's mere assertion of the relative intellectual poverty of America, and tries to explain it away with what seem to me rather puling apologies. He overlooks the fact that the disdainful Galton simply didn't know what intellectual work was being done in America. In Galton's time (1822–1911), the conditions of American life did to be sure provide chiefly non-intellectual outlets for men of ability; nevertheless, in that time America produced Emerson, Hawthorne, Thoreau, Whitman, Melville, Twain, Francis Parkman, William Hickling Prescott, Brooks and Henry Adams, William and Henry James, Emily Dickinson, Stephen Crane, Willard Gibbs, Thorstein Veblen and Charles Sanders Peirce. None of these grew up in illiterate poverty; most of them in youth led lives of studious leisure.

The slaves did grow up in illiterate poverty. All the slave states had laws making it a felony to teach a slave to read; and of the relatively few slaves who escaped, even fewer were taught to read—they didn't escape into lives of studious leisure. Before the Civil War no Southern state had public schools even for whites; after the brief period of Reconstruction the newly established public schools were deliberately starved, and the education of black children, where it was not eliminated, was made separate and deliberately inferior. Not until 1962, for example, were black teachers in the South permitted to attend the state universities. The rational hope, the transcendental clouds of glory, the sense of an open world awaiting free energy, which inspired so many white Americans, were unknown to black Americans; they knew only that their way was blocked, or that there was no way. Under such conditions it is not surprising that the country has had few black scholars or writers, and that most of those few have developed in opposition to the main currents of American thought and feeling. The sad faces of black three-year-olds, already experiencing rejection, show the continuation of that sad history; the outraged faces of black six-year-olds show the continuation of that outrageous history.

How many blacks of good genetic endowment have worn themselves out in the frustrations of an unintellectual struggle to live we will never know; how many in their bitterness and rage have turned to crime we will never know: few criminals write books. But one who did was Malcolm X; and it is instructive to put his autobiography beside Nabokov's.

All good writers give us concrete details that enable us to read their experience, however different from our own, in terms of recognizable sights, sounds, etc. One of Nabokov's memories of childhood involves a bumblebee; one of Malcolm X's involves a fly. Nabokov recalls a day when his eccentric millionaire uncle Vasily discovered in the house—"with an ecstatic moan"—a series of children's books that had delighted his own childhood:

> I see again my schoolroom . . . , the blue roses of the wallpaper, the open window. Its reflection fills the

oval mirror above the leathern couch where my uncle sits, gloating over a tattered book. A sense of security, of well-being, of summer warmth pervades my memory. That robust reality makes a ghost of the present. The mirror brims with brightness; a bumblebee has entered the room and bumps against the ceiling. Everything is as it should be, nothing will ever change, nobody will ever die.

But one of Malcolm X's early memories is of his father's funeral.

I remember that during the service a big black fly came down and landed on my father's face, and Wilfred sprang up from his chair and he shooed the fly away, and he came groping back to his chair—there were folding chairs for us to sit on—and the tears were streaming down his face. When we went by the casket, I remember that I thought that it looked as if my father's strong black face had been dusted with flour, and I wished they hadn't put on such a lot of it.

The boy who wished that was six years old.
But his "earliest vivid memory" was of a night when he was four: a memory of

being suddenly snatched awake into a frightening confusion of pistol shots and shouting and smoke and flames. My father had shouted and shot at the two white men who had set the fire and were running away. Our home was burning down around us. We were lunging and bumping and tumbling all over each other trying to escape. My mother, with the baby in her arms, just made it into the yard before the house crashed in, showering sparks. I remember we were outside in the night in our underwear, crying and yelling our heads off.

Two years later his father's skull was crushed in by people of the same kind as those who had set fire to the house. After that, Malcolm's memories were chiefly of poverty, hunger, cold, insults, condescension, crime, and prison.

The central fact of his adult life, therefore, was a metaphor he took literally. His experience of whites having been what it was, when Elijah Muhammad told him, "The white man is the devil," he believed it—in the same way that Elijah Muhammad believed it: not as a metaphorical statement but as a statement of fact. That belief suddenly made his past intelligible; and though intelligibility has nothing to do with truth, it is often more persuasive; in this case, it persuaded Malcolm X that his life had a direction and a purpose: a divinely ordained mission to fight the devil.

Elijah Muhammad had made up a whole theology to support this metaphor; though it is no *more* absurd than the popular white theology, according to which angels are white, devils are black, red, green—anything but white—and black human beings are cursed by God, it is *equally* absurd. However, if a belief is emotionally reassuring, its intellectual quality doesn't matter; and Malcolm X was reassured to the point of redemption by Elijah Muhammad's inversion of the popular white theology. In the blazing light of that new vision the particular features of individual whites were blotted out; all whites became indistinguishably evil; that is to say, Malcolm X became a racist of the most absolute kind, as insanely narrow as Hitler or Lester Maddox. He propagated a holy hatred, a black racism as indiscriminate as white racism, and as inappropriate to any particular situation in which it is applied. But gradually, as he met Muslim allies in other countries, many of whom were white, and as he became aware that some of the Black Muslim leaders in this country were using the movement for their own personal advantage— in ways that are common to all movements, of whatever kind or color—he began to perceive that not all whites were totally evil and not all blacks were totally good; he had the intellectual independence to decide that black racism was as delusive as white racism, and the moral courage to say so. But his orthodox followers, stuck in the orthodoxy he had taught them, couldn't follow him in what they regarded as treason. His father had been killed by white racists who took a metaphor literally; he himself was killed by black racists who took a metaphor literally.

Malcolm X's death, tragic in the strictest classic sense, illustrates the tragedy that is always inherent in taking literally a more general metaphor, that of "fighting fire with fire." Literally, fighting fire with fire involves burning out a zone across the path of an advancing fire, so that having advanced to that zone it can go no farther. The method is dangerous and expensive, and requires absolute control; but those who so joyfully apply it to metaphorical fires, which are no more fires than Europe is an animal or than any race is a race of devils, are more often firebugs than firefighters; and the innocents who applaud them don't appreciate the real danger, don't mind the real loss, and don't like the idea of control. Thus, for example, in the name of "fighting communism," officials at the highest levels of government have their political agents tap our phones, open our mail, censor our news, forge our signatures, break into our homes without knocking and without warrant, and imprison us, individually or en masse, without trial or even charges. But these are the very methods of communism, as of all other authoritarianisms: to the extent that the government adopts them it destroys the individual freedom it professes to defend. Likewise, in the name of "self-regulation"—i.e., of avoiding censorship— publishers, theatrical producers, movie producers and TV producers often forbid themselves to produce certain works, or pre-censor them into fatuity, rather than risk the expense of putting the onus of censorship on the censors.

And when is personal freedom not personal freedom? When the person who claims it is not a person. Every country is full of metaphorical persons. In this country most of them are actually corporations, but the law recognizes them as persons, entitled to the Fifth Amendment's protection against being deprived of life, liberty or property without due process of law—i.e., of being imprisoned, fined or hanged without trial. On these grounds the American Bankers Association campaigned against passage of the Glass-Steagall banking bill of 1933, which forbade banks of deposit to invest in common stocks—i.e., to gamble in the stock market with their depositors' money—and required them to insure their deposits up to $2,000. The A.B.A. maintained that these regulations would deprive corporate persons of their liberty. But since most of the banks in the country were then bankrupt as a result of gambling in the stock market, and most of their depositors' money had mysteriously vanished, Congress was not impressed by the A.B.A.'s fine-spun metaphor, and the bill passed. However, many other bills intended to protect the public against corporate irresponsibility have been defeated, and many that were passed have been declared unconstitutional, on the grounds that they would put metaphorical persons metaphorically in jail. Such arguments might be more impressive if those who make them didn't have such a bad record of indifference or hostility to the liberties of flesh-and-blood persons.

The problem in any human situation is how to see the flesh-and-blood persons through the dense fog of metaphors in which we live. The problem for us as English teachers is how to meet the needs of the flesh-and-blood students before us—and this sentence itself, which I am now uttering, shows how easy it is to wander into the featureless vagueness of metaphorical abstractions. We always speak of "meeting the students' needs." What needs? They have many needs. They need food, clothing and shelter. They need toothbrushes. They need medical attention. They need love. They need a sense that society needs them. They need a sense of community and non-verbal communion, as we all do; but for human beings non-verbal communion can never be fully satisfying, because it leaves unengaged and uninvolved the distinctively human element in us: our conscious mental awareness of what is going on. To take a fairly obvious example, fully human sexual love involves much more than tumescence, explosion and detumescence. Our humanity cannot be fully satisfied by the simple spasms that presumably satisfy a pair of earthworms. If it could, a casual overnight coition, without affection or sympathy, would be fully satisfying. But our nature is too complex to be fully satisfied by anything so simple. We *need* affection and sympathy. We need not only to feel but also to know that we are feeling, to understand something of what we are feeling, and to share our understanding. We need to express our feeling in words, if only to say that it is inexpressible: we need to confirm it in the one way that is peculiar to our species.

The peculiarly and distinctively human element in our nature, the differentiating overplus beyond our generic animality, the specific quality of our species, cannot be expressed without some communication of minds: we need *verbal* communication. *Homo sapiens* is the word-using species. That is our specialty, our unique potentiality. The extent to which we develop it is the extent of our functioning humanity. The adjective *infant* originally meant speechless; the generalization of its meaning from speechless to undeveloped was quite normal and natural. Not for nothing are languages and the arts that depend on language—rhetoric, literature, philosophy and history—called the humanities. Our job as teachers is to stimulate to the fullest development students who come to us with their humanistic potentialities only beginning to be developed. Their language beyond the basic necessities of practical communication being in many cases limited to a few all-purpose expletives and clichés, they try with desperate futility to achieve adequate human understanding of themselves and each other and the world through mere reduplication and intensification of their familiar non-verbal modes of communion. Their vocabulary being vague, abstract and inaccurate, they amplify their voices. They fill the gaps in their understanding with such meaningless sounds as "like" and "you know." We must give them more words and more ways of combining them. If they could cry, "Touch, touch me!" they would be poets experiencing full human awareness, an essential ingredient in full human contact; but when they come to us they can only cry "Wow!" We must not willingly let them remain so poverty-stricken. Their humanity is starved by their functional wordlessness. Being incoherent within, they seek incoherence without. Their felt need for incoherence takes various forms. In some cases, lacking love, out of communication and out of adequate human touch, they feel a need for drugs. In many cases they feel a need for endless reverberations of sound, with or without pattern or meaning, and the louder the better, lest they disintegrate. And increasing numbers of them feel a need for the consolations of religion, organized, unorganized or disorganized. Such are the realities behind the educationist abstraction "Their Felt Needs."

Obviously we as English teachers cannot and should not undertake to meet all their felt needs; in fact, our only valid function as English teachers is to try to meet a need that they all have but that most of them *don't* feel: the need for clear comprehension of the meanings and artful uses of words, without which they cannot resist the seductive insinuations and the intimidating blatancies of salesmen and saviors. Here the words "salesmen" and "saviors" are of course metaphorical. But I am aware of the fact, and so are you: I am not seducing or intimidating you, nor am I deluding myself. If our students had a similarly clear awareness of the uses and abuses of words, literal and metaphorical, they would not be so easily seduced or intimidated or deluded. There is no conflict between our pedagogical function and our social function—between our responsibility as teachers and our responsibility as citizens. We don't have to preach. If we can help the students before us to develop a feeling for the effective use of commas—not by applying invariant and often inapplicable rulebook formulas but by understanding the requirements of the particular living syntactic organism they are trying to create—we will have made a small but real contribution to vitality of thought in America. There is nothing an authoritarian fears more.

And who are the students before us, in their flesh-and-blood reality? In most cases they are young men and women at the age of maximum sexuality, so that they have a need more urgent and more important than the need to understand the artful placement of commas; in most cases, as innocent victims of John Dewey's clumsily worded and thus poorly conceived and self-deluding concern for their felt needs, they have been passively passed through high school without learning much: several chemist friends tell me that many college freshmen who have had two years of high school chemistry have no advantage over those who have had none, being equally innocent of the terminology, the valences, the atomic weights and the specific gravities; a physicist friend at one of our better universities tells me that many students in his beginning classes not only can't handle fractions but don't even know what a fraction is; and in English our remedial classes are made up entirely, and our regular freshman classes in varying degrees, of people who have got through high school and into college without being able to write in their native language a two-line memo whose meaning is clear.

Such students live in a ghetto of the mind, isolated from the intellectual life on which civilization depends, precluded from participation in society except as unconscious agents to be directed, used and abused by others, interchangeable units without distinctive qualities or special value, passive, passive, passive, even when their hottest passions are deliberately aroused and directed, a mass of expendable projectiles.

They can be used because in their uncritical innocence they are neither amused nor offended by clownish language. They are not amused but impressed by such a ridiculous jumble of metaphors as Frank Rizzo's statement about Milton Shapp, "Now that he feels the public pulse beating against his bleeding-heart philosophy he is trying desperately to change his spots." They are neither amused nor offended by the language of the Watergate conspirators, who refer to themselves and each other as "avenues," "conduits" and "facilities" and can say without smiling "It's a White House statement but not a White House position." They are not offended by the language of advertising, which seduces them with the subliminal appeal of such meaningless statements as "Canada Dry tastes like love" and "Schmidt's—the velvety soft beer, with no hard edges to get in the way of pleasure." They are not offended by the language of packaging, in which the small, medium and large sizes are called respectively "large," "giant" and "family." They don't lack brain power. They do understand that the word "large" means small. But they are not offended. The violation of language doesn't strike them as important. They don't feel it as a violation of themselves. They are not given to verbal analysis. They lack intellect. Intellect without brain power is pretentious, but brain power without intellect is helpless. It follows orders without protest. It will submit to any indignity. It will perpetrate any indignity—and all with the moral self-righteousness of Jonah sitting under the gourd vine, or of that prick in the TV commercial who refuses to have breakfast with his neighbor because the neighbor is eating something other than Total.

The largely unfelt need for intellect—for personal dignity of mind—is what we must make our students feel. They don't feel it because it is not a natural but an acquired need, a product as well as a source of civilization; and we cannot introduce our students to it by catering to their natural needs, no matter what the media merchants profess. No matter how many movies they watch or how many tapes they hear, they will not develop intellect unless they practice the art of analyzing and constructing statements: the art of verbal precision. No matter in how large a circle they hold hands, no matter how warm, firm and good the friendly pressure, no matter how sexy the non-verbal communion, no matter how gutsy the gut reaction, they will not be clearly aware of what is going on, of what they are doing and what is being done to them, unless they learn to think in words with some precision. They won't be able to resist buying the equipment. The skeptical habit is a verbal habit. There is no detachment, no independent observation, no freedom of the mind, without skill in words. An intellectual is a person who is keenly conscious of what words do. An intellectual, therefore, is a person to whom ginger ale tastes like ginger ale. That's why authoritarians are always anti-intellectuals. They owe their power to the inarticulate majority who are uncritically swept along with the crowd. Their national anthem is "Ah'm the kang of the Kansas City supermarket parkin' lot." The country-and-western strategy is insulting, but it always brings in the votes of those who don't realize that they have been insulted.

But what of the well-known phenomenon of anti-intellectual intellectuals? What of Eliot, Yeats, Lawrence, Pound, Céline, Jouhandeau, Giono, Drieu la Rochelle, d'Annunzio, Marinetti, Jünger, Hamsun,

Lagerkvist? Did they lack intellect? No. But when they enlisted their brain power in the service of authoritarian violence and fraud they disavowed their intellect. They turned it off. They made it—you should pardon the expression—"inoperative." When they wrote apologies for the suppression of independent thought they were as uncritically cheap and irresponsible as any street-corner fascist nut or radio evangelist. Consider the least nutty of them in one of his most plainly expository works. T. S. Eliot, in *Notes towards the Definition of Culture*, maintains that what is needed in the rulers of society is not superior native ability but an unquestioned assurance that they were born to rule. He therefore proposes a hierarchical society of hereditary classes, the education of whose members would be suited not to their individual qualities and capacities but to their inherited social positions. His educational proposals are strikingly similar to those of some of our contemporaries who think of themselves not as conservatives but as radicals. He would not encourage us common people to think, speak and write coherently. He would not introduce us to the grammar, diction and vocabulary that would open to us the information and ideas he would keep from us; on the contrary, he would reserve for the hereditary upper classes "the more conscious part of culture": all the disciplines necessary for understanding the history and nature of society, its institutions, and the individual soul; he would imprison us common people in "a less conscious culture": a culture of subliminal suggestions and incitements, of ritual, festival and superstition, of regional quaintness and picturesque local folkways, of provincial poverty of experience and tribal xenophobia—a culture of clichés and automatic gestures—for the purpose of keeping us docile in the alleged bliss of contented ignorance and exploitable through unthinking gut reactions. He denies "the Equality of Opportunity dogma," not by arguing but simply by asserting that there are probably no mute inglorious Miltons, that the idea that we common people have any unrealized innate capacities is a "myth," that therefore no opening up of educational opportunities or any other social change would make possible the development of talents that are now undeveloped, and that in any case, for some unspecified reason, "it might be embarrassing to have a great many Miltons and Shakespeares"—i.e., that it might be undesirable to have a great many first-rate writers. Here we have one of our certified intellectuals uttering demonstrable nuttiness.

There are vast quantities of such nuttiness. Clemenceau, reflecting on the Dreyfus affair, said, "Military justice is to justice as military music is to music"; and we, reading Clausewitz' *On War*, are tempted to say, "Military philosophy is to philosophy as military justice is to justice." What poor paltry swaggering stuff it is! Intellectually, it is on a par with heel-clicking; imaginatively, it is on a par with Ian Fleming, Mickey Spillane and Ayn Rand; ethically, it is on a par with Hitler. Nevertheless, that philosophy—a cheap theatrical glorification of violence and fraud as the most valid determinants of human affairs, and of willingness to perpetrate them as the noblest trait of human character—a monocular belief that imposing one's will on another is the highest of all human achievements and justifies any behavior whatever—has been and is being applied to civil policy in our own country by an administration at war with the young, the poor, the black, and the liberally educated; and alas, outside these categories very few people feel outraged; on the contrary, most of the inarticulate majority feel annoyed at us who remind them of the causes for outrage. They seem to share the mentality of one of Alejo Carpentier's minor characters, Sergeant Ratón, who lived in an endless dream of heroic violence, reading and rereading year after year Clausewitz' *On War* and *The Count of Monte Cristo*.

For those of us who believe in personal freedom, the

media merchants' merchandising of groupfeel and groupgut reactions, and the consequent downgrading of independent intellect, have very bad social implications. What can we as English teachers do about it? We can do our proper business as English teachers: we can make our students conscious of their language, and help them to develop some skill and range in using it. We can do them two great favors: (1) we can point out and help them to correct their errors of grammar, spelling, punctuation and vocabulary—that is to say, their imprecision of thought; (2) we can help them to develop some literary judgment. Nobody who has any functioning literary judgment can be impressed by the histrionic swagger of Clausewitz, 007, Mike Hammer, John Galt or Monte Cristo, or by the melodramatic fantasies of those who, lacking any grace or style in the use of their native language, unable therefore to think with humane grace or even with sophisticated cleverness, crudely call themselves avenues, conduits and facilities and try to use us as expendable projectiles.

2 The Body Politic

The State has its reasons, which reason knows nothing of. In practice, the term "Reasons of State" usually signifies neither rationality nor the welfare of the State, but the private interest of those in charge of government, and of the backers who put them there; nevertheless, these characters often delude themselves with the belief that their private interest is the public interest, and the public usually has too little information to know better. Moreover, the public is naturally pleased to believe that government is conducted in its interest.

This chapter will explore the metaphor of the State as an entity whose reality is superior to that of individual citizens, a whole of which they are merely a superabundance of spare parts, a body of which they are self-replacing cells, a Body Politic. The picture on the title page of Hobbes's *Leviathan* (1651) shows an idealized Charles II whose body is made up of many little people.

As far as the Western world is concerned—and alas, as we have recently become painfully aware, that's the only world most of us occidentals know anything about—the metaphor of the Body Politic began in ancient Greece and reached its fullest development in the middle ages, as a particular manifestation of the philosophic problem of universals. Later in this chapter I will discuss the medieval development in some detail, showing how it still influences our lives in ways that we are not always aware of; but first let us consider the problem of universals in some of its modern bearings on matters of race and class. Philosophy is by no means irrelevant to our daily living—even medieval philosophy.

A universal is a noun—a name—for which there is no corresponding object. That's what I say. But in the middle ages many people said it was a real thing; and quite a few people still say so in the twentieth century.

"Item."

What does an item look like? Every itemized bill lists items. The sign at the entrance to the express aisle in the supermarket says, "8 items or less." So there must be items—but just what is an item? A bag of flour is an item, a dozen eggs are an item, two pounds of apples are an item. Two bottles of ginger ale are two items, but six bottles in a carton are one item. If your mother were to say, "Bring me the item," what would you take to her? There is no such item.

"Animal."

Have you ever seen an animal? Not a dog or a bird or a crab, just an animal. There is no such animal.

"Food."

Have you ever tasted food? Not steak or potatoes or spaghetti, just food. There is no such thing as food.

"Tool."

Go into a hardware store, ask for a tool, refuse to specify further, reject all specific suggestions—saying, for example, "I don't want a hammer, I want a *tool*"; "I don't want a saw, I want a *tool*, don't you understand?"

—and see how you make out. There is no such thing as
a tool.

"Quart."

Go into a drug store and ask for a quart. "A quart of
what?" "Just a quart." "You mean a quart bottle?" "No,
I said a quart because I mean a *quart*. Don't you
understand English?" There is no such thing as a quart.

Then why do we have such words? What good are
nouns that don't signify anything in particular?

A great deal of good. They signify classes or
categories of objects, or quantities or qualities of
objects. The color red doesn't exist except in red
objects, but without the abstraction "red" we wouldn't
be able to think about those objects quite as clearly as
we do; there is no such thing as a quart, to be sure, but
when we want a certain quantity of milk or beer the
abstract word "quart" is a useful abstraction to have;
there is no such thing as furniture, to be sure, but when
we go shopping for beds, chairs and tables the abstract
word "furniture" is a useful abstraction to have. Such
words help us to organize the miscellaneous multiplicity
of things into manageable groups, classes, categories,
gradations; they help us to perceive similarities,
differences, relationships, uses, possibilities, meanings,
values: they help us to think, to convert sense
impressions into experiences, and experiences into
experience. What differentiates us from the other
animals is our superior capacity to generalize. We can't
live humanly without generalizing.

But generalizing is dangerous when it causes us to
forget the particular things about which we are
generalizing. A generalization is not a thing but the
expression of our understanding of the relationships
among things, and their quantities and qualities; a class
or category is not a thing but a certain perceived or
invented congruence among things; the name of it is an
expression of our understanding that certain things can
be appropriately grouped together: it is the result of our

grouping them together. It is a taking together, a con-ception, not a thing.

We don't get into any serious difficulty when we generalize about things, because we neither over-generalize nor under-generalize. We don't over-generalize to the extent of trying to use a tack hammer as a sledge hammer because they are both hammers an' when you've seen one hammer you've seenum all, or to use a saw and a screwdriver interchangeably because they are both tools an' when you've seen one tool you've seenum all; nor do we under-generalize to the extent of insisting that since a monkey wrench is not a hammer we couldn't use it to drive a nail if we had to. (We have definition-by-use: a monkey wrench *is* a hammer when we use it as a hammer, no matter what the dictionary says.) With regard to things, we sanely stay within the practical limits of generalization: we don't mistake abstractions for things, or things for abstractions. But with regard to human beings we do make just these mistakes; when we do, our behavior is irrational, and in its effects insane. We damage others, and in so doing we damage ourselves. We become gratuitously destructive, striking out indiscriminately against abstract fantasies and hitting real people. If that isn't insane, what is?

And we insanely justify our insane behavior. We under-generalize in failing to consider all human beings equally human. We insist that Jews, Italians, Germans, Blacks, Russians, Poles, Danes, Finns and Chinese have not only different customs but also different natures: in effect, we deny that there is among human beings a common humanity. And we over-generalize by insisting that all members of a particular race are alike in their ability and behavior, or in their inability and misbehavior. We discriminate among races but not among individuals. Baudelaire believed that all Belgians were stupid; Gobineau believed that all members of the Nordic races were aesthetically insensitive in proportion to the "purity" of their Nordic "blood." (See Chapter 8.)

Many of us, though we grudgingly or perfunctorily admit that all people are human, really believe that some are less human than others. For we tend to identify humanity with ourselves, and to regard all who differ from us in language, color, stature, proportions, manners, customs and devotions as not quite human. In World War II the German surrender was signed May 7, 1945; the first atomic bomb was exploded at Alamogordo, N.M., July 16; the next two were dropped on Hiroshima and Nagasaki August 6 and 9 respectively; so that the widespread popular misconception that we dropped them on Japan rather than on Germany for racist reasons is indeed misconceived; nevertheless it persists, both among anti-racists who disapprove and among racists who approve, because our history makes it seem plausible.[1] During World War II the United States government did in fact indiscriminately round up and put in prison camps all Japanese on the West Coast, including native-born American citizens; there was no great popular outcry against that policy; the Communist Party had nothing to say; only a few lonely liberals protested; but of course the government did not indiscriminately imprison all Germans, on the East Coast or in Detroit or anywhere else, nor did it imprison known and unabashed Nazi sympathizers unless they were convicted of particular crimes, because there would undoubtedly have been a great popular outcry against such a policy, led by conservatives for their reasons as

[1] Others' history too. Consider the following item, entitled "Hiroshima Diary," in *The New York Times* of Sunday, January 4, 1976, sec. 4, p. 7: "After the bombing of Hiroshima on Aug. 6, 1945, William Lyon Mackenzie King, the wartime Prime Minister of Canada, wrote in his diary: 'It is fortunate that the use of the bomb should have been upon the Japanese rather than upon the white races of Europe.' He described the bombing as one of 'the two great events that day,' the other being his victory in a by-election. The 1944 and 1945 diaries of Mr. Mackenzie King have been made public after a 30-year prohibition on the publication of secret Government material."

well as by liberals for theirs. In the official eyes of the United States government it was permissible to do things to Japanese, including native American Japanese, that it was not permissible to do to Germans, including native German Germans; in the official eyes of the United States government, native American citizens were not in fact entitled to the equal protection of the law. Nor were Japanese the only Americans who were discriminated against because of their race. It was common practice for German prisoners of war, en route to prison camps in the South, to be fed in restaurants to which the Black American soldiers guarding them were not admitted. This was a matter of state and local law, to which the federal government made no objection. In the official eyes of the United States government, popular notions about race were more important than the Constitution of the United States. Popular *notions?* Popular prejudices.

Since in choosing our highest officials we consult neither a genealogical stud book nor a civil service exam but our own political preferences, official policy always sooner or later reflects, however imperfectly, the preferences of the majority of us voters; and the sad fact is that we have a long record of racial prejudice. Let us consider only one item out of many that might be adduced from our popular culture. Jack London, the most popular American writer of his time, was obsessed with fear that the Chinese, aroused by the Japanese, would displace the white race as the dominant race of the world; in 1900, replying to fellow Socialists who objected to the racism he had expressed in several interviews, he said, according to his daughter, "What the devil! I am first of all a white man, and only then a Socialist!" (Joan London, *Jack London and His Times* [Seattle: University of Washington Press, 1939 and 1968], p. 284.) In one of those interviews he had said that Socialism was not devised for the happiness of all human beings but for the betterment of the white races, "so that they may survive and inherit the earth to the extinction of the lesser, weaker races." He explicitly denied that all men were brothers. (Pp. 212–13.) In 1904 he published an article, "The Yellow Peril," stating that the white and yellow races would inevitably clash in a contest for mastery of the world, and that the white race, in order to win, would have to forget its ethical principles, which in any case were nothing but an expression of its "racial egotism." (*Jack London Reports,* ed. King Hendricks and Irving Shepard [Garden City, N.Y.: Doubleday, 1970], pp. 340–50); and in 1914, in a piece of trashy science fiction entitled "The Unparalleled Invasion," he suggested that the Yellow Peril could and should be overcome by genocide. In the hot Summer of 1976, he said, the combined air fleets of Europe and America dropped all over China thin glass tubes filled with the germs of "a score of plagues" that had been "cultured in the laboratories of the West," and killed more than a billion Chinese, practically the whole population; in the cold February of 1978 military expeditions went in to kill off the few survivors, down to the last man, woman and child; then followed decontamination squads; from 1982 onward, the vacant territory that had been China was taken over by the white race, to whom it rightly belonged, and a great Renaissance followed. That was a fitting celebration of America's bicentenary. (*The Bodley Head Jack London,* ed. Arthur Calder-Marshall [4 vols.; London: The Bodley Head, 1963–66], I, 210–25.)[2]

From Jack London, whose fiction was always cheap,

[2] Adaline Glasheen reminds me that the socialist worker Jack London was by no means unique: that many victims of prejudice, including Jews, Blacks and intellectuals as well as workers and radicals, are susceptible to prejudice: "Emma Goldman (I read her autobiography) is about as anti-black as Henry Adams is anti-Semitic. She says she was reproached for it by anarchist comrades." There is no evidence that anybody reproached Henry Adams, however, and in view of the mores of his class it seems unlikely. Score one for the anarchist comrades. In this they were better than our current anti-Semitic Communist comrades.

we could expect such cheapness. Current Soviet or Russian Orthodox critics notwithstanding, he was as little a thinker as he was an artist. The problem of what we become if we permit ourselves to use any means whatever to attain our ends, and what kind of ends they become when they are attained by such means—i.e., by such people—never occurred to him; nor did the sad fact that after a while our bad habits become addictive and the means become the end—that, as George Orwell said, the purpose of war is war and the purpose of torture is torture. But somehow—centuries of experience notwithstanding—we don't expect comparable cheapness of thought from writers whom we know to have been more carefully educated—such as Henry Adams, Paul Valéry and Joseph Wood Krutch. Though we shouldn't be surprised, nevertheless we are surprised when such bargain-basement tackiness is sported by gentlemen of such self-conscious gentility. Racism is the nose-picking of aristocrats. Henry Adams's letters are spotted with anti-Semitic remarks as crude as the anti-Black remarks of Lester Maddox. Paul Valéry, being a militant anti-Dreyfusard, flunked *the* big moral test of his time—because, according to his son, "he rejected the idea that the fate of one man, whatever his merit, could be weighed in the scales against the unity and efficacy of the State." (François Valéry's preface to *History and Politics*, Vol. X of *The Collected Works of Paul Valéry*, trans. Denise Folliot and Jackson Matthews [New York: Bollingen Foundation, 1962], pp. xii–xiii.) That is to say, he accepted the idea that the interest of the State might well be served by deliberately cooking up a false charge of treason against an individual; he also accepted the idea that when the truth about the State's deliberate evil-doing becomes evident it should be suppressed. That was precisely Henry Adams's view of the Dreyfus affair: he objected to nothing but the bad public relations, the bad effect on France's reputation and influence among the nations. And Joseph Wood Krutch,

carrying further a hint thrown out by Valéry in 1922
("The European," *History and Politics,* pp. 307–23), said
with blunt explicitness in 1932—unfortunately the very
year in which Hitler came to power—something that
Valéry had been very careful to avoid actually quite
saying: that non-Europeans were for all practical
purposes not really human:

> Doubtless the possibilities of man as a biological
> organism are almost infinitely varied. Doubtless that
> organism can survive and even flourish under an
> almost infinite variety of conditions. But humanity as
> Europe knows it cannot be imagined apart from the
> social order which Europe has created, the sensibilities
> which European art has developed, and the realm of
> thought which European philosophy has set in order.
> To the taxonomist a Hottentot or a Malay may be a
> representative of the species *Homo sapiens.* But he is
> not man as man was conceived of by Descartes, and
> neither is he part of that humanity which Roman law
> proposed to save in this world and the Roman Church
> proposed to save in the next. (Joseph Wood Krutch,
> *Was Europe a Success?* [New York: Farrar & Rinehart,
> 1934], pp. 10–11; copyright © 1932 by Joseph Wood
> Krutch.)

If that paragraph means anything, it means that all
men are biological organisms—i.e., animals—but that as
far as Europe is concerned only Europeans are human,
that there is no artistic sensibility in China, Japan, Korea,
Cambodia or Siam, that there is no philosophic depth in
India, that there is no music or dance or architecture
anywhere but in Europe and its extensions, that when
you've seen one Hottentot or Malay you've seen them
all, that he is by nature outside the protection of the law,
that he has no soul or mind or personality, that he is
merely a body to be used, smaller and therefore less
valuable than that of an elephant—as the young George

Orwell observed in Burma to his gradual dismay. This kind of under-generalizing and over-generalizing is what I had in mind when I said, "We tend to identify humanity with ourselves, and to regard all who differ from us in language, color, stature, proportions, manners, customs and devotions as not quite human."

Joseph Wood Krutch was neither ignorant nor unreflective. On the contrary, he was the product of a long philosophic tradition. He was what in the middle ages would have been called a realist: a person who believed that universals were real.

That belief was first fully stated and developed by the ironic Plato, who didn't believe a word of it but whose lightness has been taken ponderously, whose poetic fictions have been misread as prosy preachments, and whose witty playing with ideas has been misconstrued into unimaginative dogmatism. The result has been an inestimable loss of intellectual pleasure in the Western world, and a disastrous weight of heaviness on the Western spirit. Since we are tracing the influence of that literal-mindedness, let us read him or rather misread him literally.

Since a true or real geometric line has no breadth or depth or thickness, Plato argued, it is invisible and unfeelable. It cannot be perceived by the eye or by the finger, nor can it be imagined in visual or tactile terms. Being without sensible qualities, it can be conceived only by pure ratiocination, as a concept or idea. It is a principle to be conceived by the mind, not perceived by the senses. But every line we draw, having unavoidable breadth and depth or thickness, is merely a crude approximation—actually a misrepresentation—of the true or real geometric line. Moreover, the misrepresentation can be erased or otherwise obliterated—it can, and in the fullness of time certainly will, cease to exist—but the true line is eternal. Therefore only the true line is real. Only the idea is real. The visible "line" is only a reflection or shadow of it. In this world our minds are imprisoned in our senses, and we perceive through them only crude approximations or shadows of truth. We see as in a glass darkly, as when we see the life of the street reflected in a store window.

Likewise, the principle or idea of the lever is eternally true, but the steel or wood in which it is temporarily embodied or manifested is not; the steel or wood will ultimately go back into the earth from which it came, but the principle of the lever is eternal; therefore the principle, not the steel or wood, is the real lever. The principle can be conceived by the mind, not seen by the eye or grasped by the hand. (The body, as we shall see in the next chapter, is just no damned good.) Similarly, the only real or true horse is the ideal horse, conceivable by the mind, not perceivable in this world.

Therefore, the way to discover the truth about anything is not by sensory observation or experiment but by pure ratiocination, proceeding logically from eternal principle to eternal principle—as in geometry, where our purpose is to demonstrate not that the angles of a particular equilateral triangle happen to be equal but that the angles of any equilateral triangle whatever *must* be equal. The way to discover the true nature of government is not to observe actual governments, which are all temporary and imperfect manifestations of it, in the same way that a triangle we draw, with its visible three-dimensional "lines," is a temporary and imperfect manifestation of the ideal or real triangle—Where was I? Ah yes: the way to discover the true nature of government is not to observe actual governments but to infer its principles by logic alone.

Plato of course understood the danger of that method: *The Republic* is a detailed and delightful dead-pan demonstration of its foolishness. His disciple Aristotle, not trusting the indirections of poetry and not being inclined to ironic play, asserted the scientific method flatly and plainly. He realized that we need abstractions and generalizations. "The particular is unintelligible," he said. But he added that the way to truth—to intelligible principles—begins with observation, comparison and classification of concrete facts in this world, that such facts are real, and that although we seek to derive from them by logical induction eternal and unchangeable principles, our knowledge of such principles is always subject to refinement and revision as we discover hitherto undiscovered facts that must be accounted for. All knowledge begins in the facts of this world. Therefore, whereas ironic Plato had said that the noun "horse" signifies an ideal reality, not the more or less imperfect reflections of it that are visible in this world, sober Aristotle said that the only real horses are those in this world, and that the noun "horse" is only a noun, a name, an abstraction, not a reality: a group name that signifies a species but is not itself a real thing. Adam had to name the animals in order to understand what he was looking at, but he didn't try to ride the word "horse."

The early medieval philosophers were all deeply influenced by Platonism, because Plato's thought on the relations of body and soul and related matters, including universals, had been infused into Christianity by a number of converted Neo-Platonists, including Saint Paul himself; whereas Aristotle's, less carefully preserved and in any case less amenable to mystical transmutation, was for a long time forgotten. But when it began to be rediscovered, in the eleventh century, it started a controversy that has continued under various names to this very day: the realist-nominalist controversy: for the new Aristotelians, who said that universals were not real things but merely *names* of genera or species—nouns for which there were no corresponding objects—called themselves nominalists.

At this point let me quote myself. I have already said as well as I can what I have to say now, and to rephrase it would be an affectation and no improvement. I therefore quote a paragraph from the first chapter of *The Sympathetic Alien: James Joyce and Catholicism* (New York: N.Y.U. Press, 1959), pp. 5–6:

The central concern of medieval philosophy was the problem of universals—whether genera and species existed independently of their individual members or were merely verbal abstractions. There is no record that the question of how many angels could dance on the point of a needle was ever considered; rather, the schoolmen asked the question, which came first, the genus *animal,* the species *horse,* or the individual horses? Just what is *equinitas?* The question is far from trivial. Are we human by virtue of our membership in the human species, or is there no such species except as a figment of the mind? Just what is *humanitas?* Our answer to this question indicates our whole social attitude. Which has priority by nature, the individual or the group? If a genus or species has objective existence, if it is a real entity and not merely a word signifying a collection of individuals, what is its nature and how is it apprehended? Is there such a thing as love, over and above particular loves? If so, what is it? Is there such a thing as justice, over and above particular just acts? If not, how do we know whether an act is just or unjust? Are there universal principles, or are there not? Are what we call principles abstracted from experience, or do they have objective existence a priori? Are they merely convenient working arrangements, subject to change with time and place, or do they have a suprahuman validity? To what extent, if any, should human affairs be governed by nonhuman standards? Should the individual be sacrificed for the principle, or vice versa? Does the organization (the government, the church, the university) exist for the sake of the individual, or the individual for the sake of the organization? Or both? Just what is their proper relationship? The relevance of such questions to our own time is obvious. Their importance and their difficulty were fully appreciated by the scholastics.

Their importance to the scholastics lay chiefly in their bearing on the proper relations between the Church and its members; the controversies that resulted were conducted in theological terms. Having discussed these matters in *The Sympathetic Alien,* I won't go into them here; but the realist-nominalist controversy also had an important bearing on the proper relations between the State and the individual: the limits of governmental authority, the extent of personal freedom, the nature of individual autonomy in society, and the nature of law.

In the twelfth century these secular matters were discussed in a great paradoxical book that has influenced political thinkers ever since—thinkers with the most diverse and conflicting views. Amid the unmannerly bruit of the schools, in which abbots and bishops freely consigned one another to Hell and William of Ockham went so far as to accuse the Pope of heresy, the coming victory of nominalism and the post-feudal conception of national unity were indicated early by the calm, gentlemanly voice of John of Salisbury. His personality also foreshadowed the urbanity of such Renaissance figures as Erasmus and Sir Thomas More. He has been compared to Milton in that he gave up a life of quiet study to enter the bull ring of politics; but there was a fundamental difference, for whereas Milton took up an uncongenial task out of a sense of duty, John of Salisbury did so out of complaisance to his friends. He was one of the most sweetly reasonable men who ever lived. A wandering scholar with no ambition but to learn, living from hand to mouth like Chaucer's Clerk of Oxenford, he accepted steady and rather dull employment because his friends persuaded him it was the reasonable thing to do. First at the Papal Curia, later at the See of Canterbury under Theobald and Thomas à

Beckett, finally as Bishop of Chartres, he was kept busy with administrative matters and political negotiations for which he had little taste: "Day and night I must transact the business of others, and can give no attention to my own interests" (Migne, *Patrologia Latina*, CXCIX, 635 D, my translation). But in such quiet intervals as he could find, including a rather happy period of exile on account of his loyalty to Thomas à Beckett, he wrote two important books: *Policraticus,* a treatise on political economy, and *Metalogicus,* a defense of logic against its enemies and against its frivolous practitioners. The first is Platonic and realistic, the second Aristotelian and half nominalistic; each in its way looks forward to the Renaissance affirmation of the worth of the individual human being.

Policraticus—The Book of the Ruler of the City, or *The Statesman's Book,* or *The Prince's Book*—is more discursive than systematic. It includes autobiography, personal complaints such as the one we have just seen, social satire, history, metaphysics, literary criticism and Biblical exegesis, all with such a rich garlanding of anecdote and classical allusion, with so many Theophrastian characters peeping out and so many quaint animals ramping through, that the over-all plan is often obscured. But there is a plan, and if the details are unproportioned they are not irrelevant. The book is divided into three parts: a denunciation of "the vanities of courts that corrupt the state," a proposal for an ideal state, and a guide to help the individual attain wisdom. The first need not detain us—we have plenty of examples of our own; the second is important for its influence on the medieval conception and even on the modern democratic conception of the State; the third is important as an indication of the coming victory of nominalism, but we need not go into it, since we already have more wisdom than we can use.

Policraticus envisions an ideal Christian society, with God at the top, the Church as minister of God's will, and the prince as minister of the Church's will in mundane affairs: "Indeed, those who minister to Him in human law are as far below those who minister to Him in divine law as things human fall below things divine" (Migne, CXCIX, 547 B). This subordination of the civil to the ecclesiastical authority is of course a reflection of John's sympathy with Thomas à Beckett and the Church in their struggle against Henry II and the State. This is not to imply, however, that John's political position determined his philosophy. He was a disciple of Cicero, which is to say of Plato at the second remove; as such, he recognized the divinity of law, and defined the prince, in contradistinction to the tyrant, as a ruler who obeys the law:

> There is therefore only this difference between a tyrant and a prince, that the latter observes the law and rules the people by its authority, and considers himself its servant. . . . For the authority of the prince depends on the authority of law; and indeed it is a greater thing than arbitrary power for a prince to put his realm under laws, so as to consider himself entitled to do nothing that conflicts with the equity of justice. [Migne, CXCIX, 513 B, 514 C.]

The question naturally follows, What is the equity of justice? What is law? The definition is purely Platonic: law is a certain fitness inherent in the nature of things, "wherefore its power extends over all things, human and divine. . . . All law is as it were a discovery, and a gift of God" (Migne, CXCIX, 514 D–515 A). All men, therefore, are bound by the law; the common notion that the prince is above the law is not true in the sense that he is permitted to be unjust or inequitable, but only in the sense that

> it should be his nature to practice equity not through fear of punishment but through love of justice, . . . and in all things to prefer the good of others before

his private will. But in public matters who can speak of the will of the prince, seeing that in public matters he may not will anything except what law or equity demands or the public interest requires? [Migne, CXCIX, 515 A.]

The prince being what by definition he is, it follows that whatsoever he does is by definition just and equitable; if he appears to be unjust his subjects have no right to complain, since in that case he is merely the instrument through which God punishes the people for their sins or tests their virtue: "Indeed, when the prince wills to be cruel to his subjects, it is not his own decision but the dispensation of God, who for His good pleasure punishes or tries them" (Migne, CXCIX, 514 A). This point is supported by the authority of Romans 13:1–2, "The powers that be are ordained of God. Whosoever therefore resisteth the power, resisteth the ordinance of God." We have here the seed of the seventeenth-century doctrine of the divine right of kings and its corollary that the king can do no wrong. Hobbes said exactly the same thing: the king is "God's lieutenant, who hath the sovereignty under God," and "representeth God's person." Nothing he does may be considered a breach of contract by his subjects, because, whether the king has seized power by force or has been chosen by covenant of his subjects one with another, he is not himself a party to any covenant and is not bound by any: "he which is made sovereign maketh no covenant with his subjects beforehand." Thus he "can do no injury to his subjects. For injury . . . is nothing else but a breach of contract; and therefore where no contracts have part, there can be no injury" (Thomas Hobbes, *Leviathan,* ed. Michael Oakeshott [Oxford, Basil Blackwell, 1960], p. 114; and *Philosophical Rudiments,* M. II, 101, quoted in *Hobbes Selections,* ed. Frederick J. E. Woodbridge [New York, Scribner's, 1930], p. 347, n. 3). This, as we shall see, is not the whole Salisburian gospel, but it is an important part of it.

As we might expect, John's ideal State is hierarchical.
Following Plutarch's exposition of the principles of
government for the Emperor Trajan (which goes back to
Republic 462)—and doubtless also Paul's conception as
stated in I Corinthians 6:15, 12:12–27, Romans 12:4 and
Ephesians 5:30—*Policraticus* compares the State to the
human body. The Church is the soul, the prince is the
head, the Senate is the heart, "whence comes the
initiation of both good and evil works" (Migne, CXCIX,
540 C). Soldiers and civil servants are the hands,
financial officers are the stomach and intestines, and
peasants are the feet. The prince's eyes, ears and tongue
are the judges and provincial governors. And so on, alas.
The proper functioning of the body depends on the
harmony and cooperation of all its members—that is to
say, on unquestioning acceptance of the "accidental
status" to which one was born, with all due deference to
one's divinely appointed superiors. "Great reverence" is
to be shown to the "ministers and friends of God," and
"even sometimes to His enemies," since "He Himself
teaches this, who often, for the greatest gentling of his
people, confers power on the worst of men" (Migne,
CXCIX, 546 D). To this injunction our author adduces I
Peter 2:13–14, 18:

> Submit yourselves to every ordinance of men for the
> Lord's sake: whether it be to the king, as supreme; or
> unto governors, as unto them that are sent by him for
> the punishment of evildoers, and for the praise of
> them that do well. . . . Servants, be subject to your
> masters with all fear; not only to the good and gentle,
> but also to the froward.

For the ruler's part, he is to make himself worthy of
reverence by administering only the law of God. He
should keep the law before his eyes at all times;
specifically, he should read it every day; he should
therefore be literate; but if he is not, let him be advised
by "literate men"—by "the prophet Nathan, and the

priest Sadoch, and by the faithful sons of the prophets, who will not suffer him to turn aside from the law of God" (Migne, CXCIX, 524 D). Which is to say that he should be guided by the Church.

Rulers who do not take divine guidance are tyrants, and are to be endured only until the Church gives the word to remove them. Starting from the orthodoxy of Romans 13, John arrives at the doctrine that rebellion to tyrants is obedience to God:

> I do not deny that tyrants are ministers of God, who by His just decree has willed them to have the primacy, whether over bodies or over souls, that through them the wicked may be punished and the good corrected and tried. . . . I will go further and say that even the tyrants of the gentiles, damned to eternal death, are ministers of God. . . . For tyrants, whom sin causes, introduces and raises up, repentance overthrows, removes and destroys.

Thus tyrannicides also are ministers of God:

> The children of Israel often served tyrants, many and various, by divine dispensation. . . . But they were permitted, when the time of the dispensation was ended, by killing the tyrants to throw the yoke off their necks; nor are those blamed through whose valor the penitent and humbled people was liberated, but a glad posterity preserves their memory as ministers of God. . . . It is just for public tyrants to be killed and the people liberated for the service of God. . . . Even priests of God hold it to be a pious act; and if it seems to have the appearance of treachery, they say it is consecrated to God by a holy mystery. [Migne, CXCIX, 785 A-B, C, D; 794 A, B; 795 A-B.]

Here we have the essence of the matter: the Church decides who is a tyrant and who isn't. The prince's sole duty is to administer the law, which "pursues the guilty without hatred of persons" (Migne, CXCIX, 515 D). The law, whose source is beyond experience, is passionless; the prince, who wields its sword, "sheds blood innocently, without becoming a man of blood; and often kills men, without incurring the name or the guilt of homicide" (Migne, CXCIX, 515 C). But since the law is a gift of God, and the Church is God's interpreter to men, "the prince receives the sword from the hand of the Church, though she herself has no sword of blood at all." The Church merely confers the power of bodily coercion on the prince,

> reserving to herself the spiritual power through the authority of the pontiffs. Thus the prince is as it were the minister of the priesthood, and exercises that part of the sacred office which seems unworthy of priestly hands. For every office concerned with sacred laws is a religious and pious office, but that is inferior which is concerned with punishing crimes, and seems to be represented most clearly by the figure of the hangman. [Migne, CXCIX, 516 A.]

John's argument is consistent within itself, but various parts of it have been used by later thinkers for the most diverse and partisan purposes. Both Charles I and Cromwell were John's heirs; Milton's justification of tyrannicide in *The Tenure of Kings and Magistrates* closely parallels the passages we have just read on that subject (*The Works of John Milton,* Frank A. Patterson, general ed. [18 vols.; New York: Columbia University Press, 1932], V, 18–25). Archbishop Laud's opposite view closely parallels the passages we have just read on the duty of subjects to obey (*Dictionary of National Biography,* XXXII, 193, col. 1). Perhaps the strangest fruit of all is the eighteenth-century American statement, variously attributed to Jefferson, Franklin, and Patrick Henry, "Rebellion to tyrants is obedience to God." Each age sees in *Policraticus* what its circumstances permit; within each age, each partisan sees in it what his predilections show him. In this it is like many other great books. In the middle ages its chief effect was to encourage political apathy; we of the twentieth century can see in it the germ of the concept of government by law rather than by caprice or "caper."

Certainly John's hierarchical society is intolerable from our modern democratic point of view, but it would be a mistake to think of him as a twentieth-century anti-democrat. We don't have to be historicists, who refrain from making ethical judgments because they mistakenly believe that all such judgments are relative to the time and place in which they are made. We can
certainly say that John's view of the human individual as a mere "member" of a political "body" involves taking a metaphor literally, that it flies in the face of the nominalist morality that recognizes the importance of individuals as such, and that it supinely acquiesces in a great deal of human suffering, individual and collective. In short, he was wrong. But that doesn't prevent our understanding why. To reject historicism is not to lose perspective; on the contrary, it is to gain perspective. The fact is that John lacked the advantage—the perspective—of being able to view himself from a distance: an ideological distance. He knew nothing of democracy, because he did not live in a democratic age; he lived in the age of the irresponsible strong man whose private will was law in his domain and whose self-interest as a rule was not enlightened. Europe was divided into hundreds of feudal estates: there were Normandy, Anjou, Lorraine and Aquitaine, Saxony, Bavaria, Württemberg and Teck, Lombardy, Savoy, Tuscany and Umbria, Castile, Navarre, Aragon and Cordova, but no France, Germany, Italy or Spain. Outside England the concept of national unity didn't exist, and the idea that a ruler was responsible to anyone but himself was all but unknown. If the political fragmentation was not matched by an equally unfortunate cultural fragmentation, it was largely because of the unifying force of the common doctrine,

common ritual and common language of the Church. The Church was thus, in fact as well as in theory, of larger scope and higher dignity than any temporal ruler. Its supremacy was challenged only in England, where the political organization was of national scope. John was neither insincere nor backward-looking; he asserted the supremacy of the Church because he was a European, as most people who lived in Europe were not—they thought of themselves as Normans or Bavarians or Lombards or Castilians—and because the Church was the only European organization. His ideal society suffered the common weakness of authoritarian societies: it did not recognize that people could differ on matters of policy without being disloyal to the State. Where all opposition is illegal, any opposition must be extreme if it is to have any effect. John could not conceive of peaceful political change. He could not conceive of reform by any means but assassination.

That was a weakness indeed. The fact that we now recognize the legal legitimacy of individuals and groups with different interests, and the necessity of means to adjust their interests by constant peaceful negotiation and change; the fact, therefore, that we now have political systems that (when they work) permit reform without recourse to violence, and the fact that no serious person openly advocates assassination, are certainly improvements.[3] The growth of personal freedom in most of Western Europe and in North America—that is, the growth and practical application of the nominalist view that the State is merely an organized collection of autonomous individuals, who have set up the organization by agreement among themselves for their mutual convenience, that they can change its rules by agreement whenever they agree to, and that it has no reality aside from such agreement, the individual

[3] This chapter was written before we found out that our own government is no better than any other in this respect.

members alone being by nature real—this is certainly an improvement—or would be if we insisted on it.

The old metaphors die hard. They change their forms and subtly persist. But form and substance are inseparable, and sometimes the new form involves a noticeable improvement of the substance—at least, it seems to. Though we no longer believe that our rulers hold office by divine appointment, we consciously or unconsciously subscribe to the metaphor, "The voice of the people is the voice of God." This, combined with the modern middle-class metaphor that God is decent, would logically seem to involve a very considerable improvement. Within rather limited limits, now and then, it does actually involve a little improvement for the time being. For though an indecent President can maintain that he has "a mandate from the people" to disobey the law and ignore its procedures, and though his former chief adviser on domestic policy can publicly refuse to say that that mandate would not justify murder, and though the President can subsequently go on TV and appeal to "the people" to short-circuit the law for him, we sometimes temporarily refuse to lift our godlike voice and authorize him to nullify our lawful institutions in order to punish us for our sins or test our virtue. We insist that he resign and appoint a successor, whom we then passively permit to ignore the law, to open our mail, etc.

Logically, it would seem to be inconceivable that any elected official, or the appointee of any elected official, has God's mandate to ignore God's law, or to punish or test God. But we seldom insist on logic. As long as our rulers' prejudices confirm our own, we permissively permit them to do pretty much as they please. We are not yet accustomed to the theoretical advantages of representative government. We don't yet quite believe in them. We have a long tradition of being abused and obedient. Historically, we lack self-esteem. The next chapter will deal with one of the reasons.

3

The Beastly Body
and the Irrational Female

The notion that the body is inferior to the soul, and the notion that women are inferior to men, have always reinforced each other; the exploitation of women as servants, items of décor and unloved sex objects has always been excused by the notion that they are not rational, that their behavior is ruled by emotion, instinct, intuition, impulse, whim—that they are essentially mindless bodies—and has been reinforced by the notion that the only proper function of the body is to serve the soul during its brief exile in this world. Plato's Socrates made an absolute separation between love and lust. Love, he said, involved intelligent conversation, a mingling of souls; since women were incapable of intelligent conversation, they were to be regarded as breeding stock merely, and Platonic love was love between men—at its best in old age, when the soul was free at last of the body's importunities.

The connection between the two notions was first made explicit, so far as I know, by John Scotus Erigena

(c. 830–c. 880) in his heretical book *De Divisione Naturae*.[1]
Adam fell before he was tempted, said Erigena; Eve was
the result, not the cause, of his fall. His will was
perfectly free; the fall was due to an error of judgment,
the intellectual darkness in which, according to all good
Platonists, all sin consists. The story of his expulsion
from Paradise was merely an allegorical representation of
his self-expulsion from the spiritual Paradise of
communion with the Godhead:

> Man fell by himself rather than by the Devil's
> temptation; and moreover it was not in Paradise but
> while descending from it, while deserting by his own
> free will the felicity of Paradise—that is to say, the
> vision of peace—and while falling into this world that
> he was smitten by the Devil and robbed of
> blessedness. Nor indeed is it credible that man could
> both remain in contemplation of the eternal peace and
> be persuaded to fall from it by woman (corrupted by
> the serpent's venom). [Migne, *Patrologia Latina,* CXXII,
> 811 C-D. My translation.]

Erigena, a Dionysian Neo-Platonist, believed that all
things flow from the divine Unity or Godhead, become
less and less integral as they recede from the center, and
in the fullness of time regain their integrity as they
reapproach it. All motions—departure, wandering,
returning—are undertaken freely, without compulsion.
The damned departed freely; they can and will ultimately
return freely; being damned is a matter of being wrong,
a state into which nobody falls except by misjudgment
and in which nobody remains when once he sees his
error; therefore even Satan, who strayed first and

[1] My colleague Jane Tompkins writes, "In your phrase 'first . . .
explicit' connection between the inferiority of women and of the body,
do you mean non-mythic, discursive? I seem to remember that sky
gods are often male, earth gods female; to some that language would
seem explicit enough." It does indeed.

wandered farthest, will ultimately return to God. Adam likewise, following impulse rather than reason, freely and of his own accord turned away. The sleep *(dormitio)* into which he was thrown was an outward manifestation, for his and our instruction, of the drowsiness *(sopor)* of his soul both before and after it fell into error; the creation of Eve from his side was an outward manifestation of his loss of spiritual wholeness *(integritas):*

And thus he was split into two sexes, masculine and feminine: which splitting took its cause not from nature but from vice. . . . That drowsiness was both the cause and the result of sin. . . . Whence we observe that Scripture introduces the feminine condition *(conditionem mulieris)* after Adam has fallen asleep, thereby intimating to us that if human nature had not by the irrational motion of its free will abandoned the simple and full integrity with which it was constituted in the image of God, but had remained always in unchanging contemplation of truth, it would by no means have become liable to splitting into two sexes as are the irrational animals, but would be multiplied in its own way, as the number of angels is multiplied, without sex. [Migne, *P.L.,* CXXII, 817 D, 835 C–836 B.]

Christ, the second Adam, said Erigena, was in his human aspect as uncorrupted as the first had been before the fall: "In the first Adam nature is split into masculine and feminine; in the second it is made one. In Jesus Christ is neither masculine nor feminine. In the first, universal nature is expelled from the felicity of Paradise; in the second, it is recalled and restored to that felicity" (Migne, *P.L.,* CXXII, 836 C). And since the resurrection of Christ prefigures the ultimate resurrection of the whole human race in "the simplicity of pristine nature," without all the unworthy superadditions incurred through Adam's sin, it is not to be believed that the sexual organs will be resurrected (Migne, *P.L.,* CXXII, 836 D–837 C).

Erigena was heretical in his conclusions, but perfectly orthodox in his assumption that sex is shameful, and perfectly in accord with the popular masculine belief that "the feminine condition" also is shameful.

That belief has persisted with unbroken continuity down to our own time. Toward the end of the Renaissance, the failure to achieve human perfection was represented in Milton's Adam and Eve; toward what may be the end of the modern world, the failure to achieve human perfection is represented in Samuel Beckett's Murphy and Celia (*Murphy* [Routledge, 1938; Grove Press, 1957]). The two couples are not so dissimilar as they may seem.

In Milton's Paradise the sexes were "not equal":

For contemplation hee and valour formd,
For softness shee and sweet attractive Grace,
Hee for God only, shee for God in him:

he for "absolute rule," she for "subjection" and "coy submission" (*Paradise Lost,* IV, 297–311). Eve gladly accepted the arrangement, since, as she told Adam, she recognized the subsidiary nature of her nature:

O thou for whom
And from whom I was formed flesh of thy flesh,
And without whom am to no end, my Guide
And Head. [IV, 440–43.]

She was at first enamored of her own beauty reflected in a pool, she said; but when God's voice led her to Adam and he seized her hand, she saw immediately

How beauty is excelld by manly grace
And wisdom, which alone is truly fair. [IV, 490–91.]

Therefore,

> My Author and Disposer, what thou bidst
> Unargu'd I obey; so God ordains,
> God is thy law, thou mine: to know no more
> Is womans happiest knowledge and her praise. [IV,
>   635–38.]

Beckett's Murphy and Celia are a roughly analogous
pair. Murphy is formed for contemplation and valor:
when he is at his best in godlike seclusion, his mind
contemplates itself contemplating itself and loves itself
with the intellectual love with which Spinoza's God loves
himself (Grove Press ed., pp. 107–13); when he is at his
best in the outer world, he contrives—by ruse, rhetoric,
play-acting and an unaccountable personal magnetism—
to defraud of a little more than a penny a "colossal . . .
plutomanic" corporation "highly endowed with the
ruthless cunning of the sane." He does it just as a matter
of principle (pp. 80–84.) Celia being little more than a
body (p. 10), she appeals to the part of Murphy that he
hates, and distracts him from the part that he loves (p.
8); he doesn't appreciate her love, generosity,
conscientiousness and absolute self-abnegation; however,
since she supports him with the earnings of her
prostitution, he accepts the arrangement as long as she
does. Only when she wants him to find work so that she
can give up hers does he consider it stupid and
intolerable. Thus, through whatever metamorphoses, the
notion that sex is shameful, and the allied notion that
women cannot be treated as equals, persist.

In the middle ages, however, it was widely believed
that women could emancipate themselves from the
feminine condition by forswearing sex; and that belief
also was rooted in the history of philosophy.

When an ancient Greek recovered from an illness, he
expressed his gratitude by offering a cock to Asclepius.
Whether or not he thought the god needed his gift, the

act—as sacrifice or convention or both—was undoubtedly good for the patient, being in some cases perhaps a necessary part of the cure. Socrates's dying words—"I owe a cock to Asclepius"—were a consummate paradox that stood Greek culture on its head.

It seems to me that he had no such intention, that he was being ironical, and that his disciple Plato, aware of his ironic humor and quoting him without comment, was being doubly ironical. But that is not the way Plato has been read. His editors and commentators have unfortunately presented him not as an outrageous maker of modest proposals but as a doctrinaire authoritarian of the most unimaginative kind. Bound by their own preconceptions, they have taken his urbanely humorous fictions humorlessly and literally. He was a gentleman, and they have made him an exhorter; he was a subtle poet, and they have made him a preachy propagandist.

It's too bad. With regard to everything else, I have learned to live unperturbed and quietly resigned to the fact that I am uniquely right in a world of error; but it's really too bad that I am uniquely right with regard to the interpretation of Plato.[2] For all those generations of

[2] Since writing this chapter I have read Huizinga's *Homo Ludens* (the Beacon Press paperback edition). In Chapter IX, "Play-Forms in Philosophy," Huizinga comes close to my conception, especially on pp. 49–51. "The dialogue is an art-form, a fiction," he says; "for obviously real conversation, however polished it may have been with the Greeks, could never have had the gloss of literary dialogue. In Plato's hands it is a light, airy thing, quite artificial" (p. 50). He gives a number of examples. When I read this to my wife she reminded me that John Stuart Mill, in the *Autobiography* (New York: New American Library, 1964, p. 38), doubts that Plato himself regarded his works "as anything more than poetic fancies." And now I recall that Milton, in *Areopagitica*, wishes it were possible to excuse Plato's *Laws* as having flowed from "the genial cups of an Academic night-sitting"; and that Ezra Pound, in *Guide to Kulchur*, says the germ of the comedy of manners is in Plato's dialogues. I have indicated the method that led to my own conclusion —that the dialogues are modest proposals in Swift's sense—in two brief passages on *Phaedrus:* (1) in *Matters of Style*, p. 21, and (2) in *The Irrelevant English Teacher*, p. 132. Close analysis of *The Republic* would reveal similar ironies from beginning to end.

wrongos from Saint Paul onward have made their
misconceived Platonism an important element in
Christianity and thus a major influence on Western
philosophy, literature, government and daily life; and
their misconception—which Jesus had no more to do
with than Plato—has alienated the souls of Western men
and women from their bodies.

Consider.

Egfrid, King of Northumbria from 670 to 685, was
one kind of man for his first wife and quite a different
kind for his second. During the reign of the first,
Ethelthryth, he was terrible in battle but cowed in his
own home: she lived with him twelve years without once
granting him access to her bed. During the more
reasonable administration of the second, Eormenburh,
who gave him a son, he lost his fierceness—and his
battles.

We owe this glimpse into his character to the
Venerable Bede's habit of checking everything that went
into his *Ecclesiastical History of the English People*. Having
heard the story, which "certain had come to doubt," of
the Queen's twelve years of sexless marriage, he checked
with a man who might have some information: Wilfrid,
the King's former bishop. Yes, said Wilfrid,

> . . . he could be a very sure witness of her virginity,
> for so much as King Egfrid promised to give him
> lands and much money if he could persuade the
> Queen to use his company, because he knew that she
> loved no man in the world more than him [i.e., than
> Wilfrid] (trans. J. E. King, *Baedae Opera Historica* [2
> vols.; Loeb Classical Library, II, 103]).

What Wilfrid's answer was, Bede doesn't say; but in
any case Ethelthryth continued to reject the King and
finally prevailed on him to let the marriage be annulled
so she could become a nun; Wilfrid invested her with the
veil, and the King divested him of his bishopric and
imprisoned him for nine months.

We owe the story of Egfrid's subsequent successes in bed and defeats in battle to William of Malmesbury's *De Gestis Pontificum Anglorum* (ed. Thomas D. Hardy [London: English Historical Society, Rolls Series, 1840], pp. 219–20). Malmesbury, who was not a Freudian, did indeed see a relationship of cause and effect here, but attributed it to divine displeasure. Think about this for a while and see where you come out.[3]

Ethelthryth's life as a nun was exemplary. After a year in a convent at Coldingham she became Abbess of Ely. She seldom ate more than once a day, never wore anything but itchy wool next to her skin, and permitted herself only three baths a year, in honor of Easter, Whitsuntide and Twelfthtide. On such occasions, she who had been a princess and a queen bathed the other nuns first. Her death resulted from an infection of the jaw and neck, which she attributed to the fact that in her girlhood she had taken pleasure in necklaces. She welcomed the sickness with "great joy," saying, "I believe that the heavenly pity hath therefore willed me to be grieved with the pain in my neck, that so I may be acquitted from the guilt of superfluous vanity" (*Baedae Opera Historica,* II, 109, 111).

There was a woman ridden by an idea, and a crazy

[3] Adaline Glasheen writes, "Do you know Bradford's journal?—very self-righteous account of how they put to death pilgrims who coupled with animals—and also the animals. I mention this (the animals dead always strike me as a peculiar refinement) because your horrid examples are usually Roman Catholic and I'd like to see you spread your horrors around. Did you ever, for instance, read about Thomas Harris' sexual utopia?" I hadn't, but I looked it up. Harris was a Swedenborgian and a swindler, who advocated celibacy in marriage but recommended that men who couldn't "contain" should keep mistresses. He didn't recommend boyfriends for women. For an account of his nutty community at Brocton, N.Y., see John Humphrey Noyes, *History of American Socialisms* (Dover paperback reprint), pp. 577–94; for an account of Harris's swindling, see Mark Holloway, *Heavens on Earth: Utopian Communities in America, 1680–1880* (Dover paperback reprint), pp. 215–16. And consider the grimly amusing wedding night of the Presbyterian Colwans in James Hogg's novel *The Private Memoirs and Confessions of a Justified Sinner.*

idea at that. The fact that it was not considered crazy in the middle ages doesn't affect its quality: the middle ages were a crazy period. I would not go so far as to say that our own period is sane, but much of its insanity consists in clinging to essentially the same idea that maddened the middle ages—the dissociation of body and soul—and for various reasons a smaller proportion of people now cling to that idea. The result is an improvement: now there are more and larger islands of sanity in the wild sea of madness.

Let me give you a few more illustrations from the middle ages and the decline of the Roman Empire, when that particular madness took its most obvious forms.

Egfrid's contemporary Aldhelm, Abbot of Malmesbury and Bishop of Sherburne (639–709), was by no means an ignorant hysteric such as would be impressed by a Billy Graham or a Maharaj Ji. He was a highly literate hysteric. He had the best education his age afforded; and if that was less in quantity and poorer in quality than happier ages before and after afforded, still it was considerable. But because he was unable and unwilling to reconcile his soul to his body, he was subject to intellectual fidgets in which the flesh was made word. In the Latin riddles he wrote by way of mental exercise, the sexual imagery looks forward to that of Bosch and Breughel. In one (No. 84), what seems to be a pregnant sow turns out to be a metrical syzygy. That is not the product of a happily occupied mind. In another (No. 80) he consciously or unconsciously compares a drinking glass to a woman, and a drunkard's physical fall to a sensual man's moral fall. The glass speaks:

> Yea, many long to hold me in their hand,
> Fingering my slippery shape in dainty grasp;
> But I befool their minds, the while I lay
> Sweet kisses on their lips that press me close,
> And urge their tottering footsteps to a fall.

[*The Riddles of Aldhelm,* trans. James Hall Pitman, (New Haven: Yale University Press, 1925).]

In Aldhelm's well-stored and humorous mind religious orthodoxy seems to have produced a tendency to regard all life as a tissue of contradictions. This tendency is seen in his attitude toward sex, a major preoccupation of serious thinkers in the middle ages. As a young monk, says William of Malmesbury,

To overcome the strength of the body's rebellion, he immersed himself shoulder-deep in a spring near the monastery. There, regarding neither the icy coldness in Winter nor the vapors that rose from that marshy place in Summer, he passed his nights without offense. He also imposed on himself the task of singing through the whole Psalter while there. . . . If at any time he was tempted by the lust of the body, not only did he deny its allurements but often won a notable victory over it. For at no time did he refuse the company of women in order to escape, as others do, who fear opportunity. On the contrary, whether they were sitting or lying, he lingered in their presence until his flesh grew dangerously warm; then he departed, quiet and unmoved in spirit. The devil saw and laughed, resolving at some other time to join him to a woman and divert his mind from his insistent psalm-singing. But he prevailed against the women, and with perfect modesty preserved his chastity. The trouble of his flesh, however, remained; the evil spirit tormented him with wantonness. To the truth of my assertions as to how much he cherished the love of celibacy, his excellent books *On Virginity* bear witness —those books in which he sets forth its honor, adorns its beauty, and crowns its constancy. Nor is it on any account to be believed that the holy man did otherwise than as he taught, or lived otherwise than as he advised. (*De Gestis Pontificum Anglorum*, pp. 357–58.)

Aldhelm's was by no means a unique preoccupation. Robert Mannyng of Brunne (1260–1340), in *Handlyng Synne,* a handbook of virtues and vices, translated from William of Wadington's *Manuel des Pechiez,* tells how Saint Benedict (480–543), praying one day in his cell, was tempted by a devil who came to him in the pleasant and innocent form of a bird—a throstle. As the bird sat near him, singing merrily, Benedict blessed it; but when he made the sign of the Cross, the bird disappeared. Immediately the saint was shaken with "so grete temptyng of lechery" as he had never experienced in all his life. The vision of a fair woman filled his inward eye, and the thought of her almost drove out the thought of God. He was tempted to leave his hermitage, but by the help of the Holy Ghost he overcame the devil: he threw off his clothes and rolled naked among the thorns and nettles that grew outside his cell, "Tyl hys temptacyun was al gone" (*Robert of Brunne's "Handlyng Synne," . . . With Parts of William of Wadington's "Manuel des Pechiez,"* ed. Frederick J. Furnivall [Early English Text Society, No. 119; London, 1901], pp. 238–40).

Whether such stories were historically true or not makes no difference; they were and are psychologically true. Aelfric the Grammarian (c. 955–c. 1020–25), the best and most prolific English writer of his time, wrote homilies and translated into West Saxon a number of saints' lives, drawn from such earlier sources as Augustine, Jerome, Gregory the Great, Bede and Smaragdus, in which he recounted many legendary struggles for virginity. The life of "St. Eugenia, Virgin," is typical. Eugenia, daughter of Philip, the pagan ruler of Alexandria under the Emperor Commodus, was instructed in "Greek philosophy and Latin eloquence"; but discovering the doctrines of St. Paul, she determined to become a Christian. Accordingly, she disguised herself as a man, and with her two servants, the eunuchs Protus and Jacinctus, fled from Alexandria to a nearby community of Christians. God revealed her intention and her identity to the leader of the community, Bishop Helenus, who welcomed her, telling her

> how she, by the virginity which she had chosen,
> greatly pleased the heavenly King;
> and said, that she should extremely suffer
>   persecutions
> because of her virginity, and should yet be preserved
> by the help of the true Lord, who shields his chosen
>   ones.

[*Aelfric's Lives of Saints*, ed. Walter W. Skeat, (Early English Text Society, No. 76; London, 1881), pp. 29, 31.] As it turned out, she was persecuted not for her virginity but for her Christianity; the two seem to be so closely related in the author's mind that they are practically identical—though surely as a student of theology he knew better.

At home her parents were in great distress, thinking they had lost her; but—like so many people who serve ideals transcending concrete human relationships—she was not disturbed by their grief. She had disavowed their values and them. Having been baptized, she and her servants became permanent members of the Christian community; her secret was not revealed, and her conduct was so exemplary that when Bishop Helenus died she was chosen to replace him as leader of the community.

> Then the Almighty Ruler granted her
> that she might heal infirm men, [i.e., human beings,]
> whom ever she visited as they lay in sickness.
> She drove away also foul devils
> from persecuted men, through the true faith. [P. 33.]

It was this power that led to the revelation of her secret. One of her patients, a widow named Melantia (Blackness), was sexually aroused by the supposed young

man, and, "wholly filled with evil," urged Eugenia to
marry her:

> "I ween it is no unrighteousness before God
> that thou shouldst enjoy a wife and happiness in this life."
> Then Eugenia replied to this flattery,
> and spake to the woman to this intent,
> that the desires of the present world
> are extremely deceitful, though they be pleasant,
> and the lusts of the body oftentimes seduce
> and bring them to sorrow who love them most.
> [P. 35.]

In the midst of such exhortations Melantia embraced
Eugenia, hoping to seduce her; Eugenia pulled away and
fled, reproaching herself as an instrument of the devil; and
Melantia, like Potiphar's wife and God knows how many
others, went to the authorities and charged her scorner with
attempted rape.[4] The chief authority was—of course! of
course!—Philip, Eugenia's father. He had her arrested and
brought before him. Faced with an array of perjured
witnesses who backed up Melantia's story, Eugenia could
clear herself only by revealing her sex and her identity.
Apparently there was just one way to do it:

> ... she tare apart her robes,
> and revealed her breast to the angry Philip,
> and said to him, "Thou art my father!" [P. 39.]

[4] I read this chapter to the Women's Faculty Club of the University of
Pennsylvania, to get their reactions. Many of them objected to this
statement, especially to the implications of the clause "and God knows how
many others." None defended it. The objection is well taken. Of course I
don't believe that women who say they have been raped are playing games
—certainly not in the vast majority of cases. But, as I pointed out, the
statement is based on John D. Yohannan's anthology *Joseph and Potiphar's
Wife in World Literature: An Anthology of the Story of the Chaste Youth and the Lustful
Stepmother* (New Directions, 1968). He gives some dozen examples from all
around the world and from ancient times to the present. "But all those
stories were written by men," said one of my auditors. They were.

This was essentially the technique of Aldous Huxley, who denounced sex while dishing it up; on a somewhat lower artistic level, the confession magazines do the same thing—a coy salacity being the tribute literary priggishness pays to its audience. The torturing of naked women is as much a convention of martyrologies as of modern schlock novels; the moral superiority of the schlock novels to the martyrologies, and of the pubic-hair magazines to the confession magazines, lies in the fact that they don't moralize; but they are no better in that they too consider sex dirty.

The intensity of the medieval devotion to the ideal, the low esteem in which merely temporal relationships were held, is indicated by Eugenia's defiant statement to her father and brothers—a statement in which she included her absent mother:

"I, for Christ's love, abandoned you all,
and despised as dung the lusts of the world." [P. 39.]

Her parents and brothers, however, welcomed her back with joy and became Christians, converting many others by their example. Philip interceded for the Christians with the new Emperor, Severus, who put a stop to the persecutions. Shortly afterwards Philip was made Bishop of Alexandria; but the heathen having poisoned Severus' mind against him, he was secretly assassinated, by imperial decree. Then Eugenia went to Rome, with her mother, brothers, and servants. They were at first well received, and made many converts to Christianity; but when one of the converts, having chosen a life of virginity, refused to marry a friend of the Emperor, she was cut in two and the persecution of Christians was resumed. Protus and Jacinctus, the eunuchs, were beheaded—

and quickly they departed victoriously to Christ.
These martyrs were never, throughout their lives,

defiled with women, but continued in purity
unto their lives' end, with much faith. [P. 47.]

Apparently it was better even to be a eunuch than to
lead the life of a normally sensuous person. Next
Eugenia was arrested, dragged to the temple of Diana,
and commanded to worship the goddess. Instead, she
prayed

> to the Almighty God,
> and the temple of the devil fell utterly to the ground,
> and sank into the earth, with all its idols. [P. 49.]

Then she was thrown into the river with a stone hung
from her neck, but

> the stone brake in twain, and she sat upon the water.
> [P. 49.]

Efforts to kill her by burning, boiling and starvation were
equally unsuccessful: Christ quenched the flames, cooled
the water, and visited her in the dark dungeon, bringing
her heavenly light and a snow-white loaf of bread.
Finally, with Christ's consent, she was martyred on
Christmas Day; her mother joined her in Heaven a week
later, and when her brothers died the whole family was
joyously reunited. (If you go for this kind of thing, and
want some more, look up Cynewulf's version of the life
of St. Juliana, in *The Exeter Book,* Part I, trans. Israel
Gollancz, [Early English Text Society, No. 104; London,
1895]. You will find it very helpful in case you are
plunged into a vat of melted lead, for example.)

Here we see all worldly values reversed: not only
wealth and social position, but also marriage, children
and familial affection—all the things people normally
desire—are despised as dung; poverty, exile, celibacy,
and death in prison are gladly embraced. This reversal is
manifest in all Aelfric's homilies and saints' lives. In the

life of "Saint Basilius, Bishop," a girl who wanted to
marry was told by her father,

> "I desired through chastity to wed thee to Christ,
> to the company of angels, for the comfort of my soul,
> and thou thus madly desirest a husband." [P. 75.]

In the "Passion of Julian and his Wife Basilissa," the
young couple on their wedding night, lying in bed
together, vowed perpetual virginity; Christ came down
from Heaven to congratulate them personally, and the
bed shook with the momentousness of the occasion.

> Thus Julian kept his bride unpolluted

and they were

> counted among the unsullied saints. [P. 95.]

In "Saint Agnes, Virgin," a maiden wooed by the son
of the Prefect of Rome chose death rather than
marriage. After she was killed "with death-bearing
sword,"

> her father and mother, with great joy,
> took her body, and brought it to their own house,
> and buried her there without sorrowing. [P. 185.]

The Emperor Constantine's daughter Constantia, stirred
by Agnes's example, consented for political reasons to
be betrothed to the heathen general Gallicanus, but
prayed that before the wedding day Christ would make
him see the wickedness of heathendom and of
matrimony. Realizing that God helps those who help
themselves, she planted two secret Christian missionaries
in his entourage when he went away on a campaign, and
her prayer was answered: Gallicanus was converted to
Christianity, swore never to marry, gave away his estates,

became a monk and later a hermit, was slain in the desert by a heathen, and

departed victoriously to Christ. [P. 193.]

Marriage is pollution and sullying, death is victory, and the world is well lost: the themes of Aelfric's discourse were the most common themes of medieval literature. Before his time there were already many homilies to the same purport, drawn from the same sources. The best known of these are the Blickling Homilies, so called because they were discovered in the library of Blickling Hall, Norfolk. The manuscript was written in 971, but the homilies were apparently composed in the time of King Alfred (849–99), since their language is that of the late ninth and early tenth centuries. The first homily, on the Annunciation, deals with the mystery and glory of virgin birth, the praise of virginity, and the depreciation of ordinary, or sinful, procreation. That the writer's mind is obsessed with sex is evident in every paragraph. He protests much too much. The writing of homilies seems to have been a legitimate way of expressing one's preoccupation with a forbidden subject.

These examples should be enough to hold us for a while. The question is, Why was the subject forbidden? Why was sex, even in marriage, considered a pollution? Why was the life of the body considered not something to enjoy but something to be suppressed insofar as possible? I have chosen examples from the middle ages because they present the dissociation of body and soul in its most extreme forms, unmodified, undissimulated, unabashed; but in less obvious forms it underlies all subsequent conceptions of human nature that have prevailed in Europe and America.

Falstaff's first line on stage is, "Well, Hal, what time of day is it, lad?" But what real satyr ever thought of time? The question is inconsistent with the man's public character, as Hal instantly recognizes; and the inconsistency is not accidental but rooted in history. Great Pan is dead: he died the night Plato was born of a virgin: Falstaff comes not fourteen hundred but seventeen hundred years too late. For all his sensuality, he is not at home as the pre-Platonic Greeks were at home with the delights of the flesh. He cannot enjoy them in innocence, because they are no longer considered to be innocent. The earlier Greeks did not think of Pan or Aphrodite or Dionysus as evil, but ironic Plato modestly proposed to let no poets sing them in his ideal society—a society he mocked with—shall I say it? well, yes—with dead-pan humor because he saw that the old free culture of Athens was too free for a timid generation who would welcome a dictator, as in fact they did; the suppression he had recommended mockingly was taken seriously by his successors, and when Christianity became the official religion of the Roman Empire a humorless Platonism that would have appalled Plato laid its heavy hand on literature. Only fragments of Sappho, Anacreon and Alcaeus survived the cleansing fires of the triumphant Church. In those fires love was transmuted into lust, conviviality into drunkenness, the pleasures of the table into gluttony, ease into sloth, the social amenities into cozenage and hypocrisy. The flesh being forbidden, its children became outlaws. Falstaff is obsessed with a feeling of guilt; therefore he is not free and easy in his address, but insolent, defiant, and vulgarly aggressive. His life is a never-ending war with society—a society whose values, however, he thoughtlessly accepts; therefore he is at war with himself. Allusions to hanging and whipping make him melancholy —not angry, not fearful, for he knows he is not liable to them, but melancholy, for he feels that he deserves them. He is no rebel, but merely a delinquent. However jestingly, he wishes he had a good name; however flippantly, he promises to reform; he concedes that the old councilman who berated him in the street was right; he even justifies highway robbery in terms of middle-class virtue and moral rectitude. This is a quibbling, uneasy, latter-day, indoor sort of paganism, not amoral but immoral, not healthy but diseased, corrupt, insane.

The misinterpreters of Plato did this to us. Denying the physicality of the mind and the intelligence of the body, they cut us in two, they divorced us from ourselves. They made us ashamed of our bodies. Thanks to them, we are all more or less self-conscious in the enjoyment of our appetites. The Wife of Bath cannot take her sexual enthusiasm as a matter of course, but feels impelled to convince her chance companions that she is right and they are wrong; she assumes an attitude of mocking defiance that lends the recital of her adventures a charming vulgarity. In pre-Platonic Greece such a character could not have been conceived. Between her too much protesting and Agamemnon's frank matter-of-fact statement that he prefers Chryseis to his wife, the difference is so profound that if the two characters should meet in some literary afterworld they would be utterly unable to understand each other. Nor would Iphigeneia, lamenting that she is "wife of no man and mother of no child," understand Britomart's making a career of virginity. Alcestis piteously takes leave of her marriage bed; the lady of Milton's ninth sonnet chooses "the better part" of not marrying.

The ascetic tradition, so strong and positive in the middle ages, is still with us in more tactful and negative ways. Saint Severinus of Noricum, who would not kiss a healthy woman, kissed the rotting flesh of leprosy in a man—and his choice was considered not perverse but meritorious. Heinrich Suso thought to win merit in the sight of God by wearing tight leather pants lined with sharp bits of brass that caused festering sores. If that isn't crazy, what is? But he wasn't considered crazy by his crazy society. This is not relativism. It is an assertion

that medieval society was crazier than modern society—
i.e., that one society is better than another, the standard
of value being the individual person. A society is better
or worse according as the lives of proportionally more or
fewer people are healthy, happy, peaceful, productive,
and on occasion joyful. The middle ages were full of
crazy misdirected heroism and strength of will that made
the world worse rather than better. Though we no
longer encourage such extremes of mortification, the
basic notion that the pleasures of the flesh are somehow
undesirable still influences our thought and makes our
world unnecessarily grim. It underlies every conservative
government. It underlies all our private grimnesses: our
cold showers, our carrot eating, our milk drinking, our
thirty-mile hikes, our community sings, our prayer
breakfasts, our John Birch meetings and all the other
uplift activities we condemn ourselves to.

From time to time we rebel against the notion, but
the very form of our rebellion—not denial but defiance,
not indifference but counter-urgency—indicates our
continuing acceptance of it: thus the Restoration
comedy's self-conscious immorality did not deny that sex
was immoral, and our current self-conscious dirtiness
does not deny that sex is dirty: in each case we have a
willed decision to do something we really fear we
shouldn't do. The problem is how to emancipate
ourselves from that fear: how to reunite the too long
dissociated body and soul.

I don't know the answer. But I do believe that if we
become more clearly aware of the metaphors we live by
—the pure intellect, the beastly body, the beastly people,
the beastly bourgeois, the body politic, etc.—though we
may still not be able to solve the problem, we will be
able to have more fun living with it.

4

The Beastly People

Alexander Hamilton was neither the first nor the last to call us, the people, a beast. That metaphor is ancient, medieval, Renaissance, and all varieties of modern; it seems to have occurred in all literate societies, and doubtless it has occurred in illiterate, pre-literate and post-literate societies.[1]

[1] Here, for example, is part of John Gower's analysis (c. 1382) of the Peasants' Revolt of 1381. The peasants, he said, were "asses rebellious against the halter and the burden, . . . oxen, who refused any longer to be subject to the yoke and who would no longer eat straw, . . . swine, furious and possessed by the devil, . . . not content with acorns for their food or water for their drink; they devour rich food in the city and drink good wine, so that they lie in their drunkenness as dead. They despise the pig-stye and defile kings' palaces with their filth. . . . Dogs, who are not content with the food from their master's table, but range in search of better. . . . Here are Cut and Cur from their wretched kennels. . . . The one-eyed is there and the three-legged dog limps behind barking. These cannot be soothed by stroking, but bare their teeth in anger against you" (*Vox Clamantis,* in *The Complete Works of John Gower,* ed. and trans. G. C. Macaulay [4 vols., Oxford: Clarendon Press, 1899–1902], IV, xxxv–xxxvi). It never occurred to him that they had revolted not only against poverty but also against *superbia.*

In some cases—since authoritarians distrust discussion —the metaphor includes the adjective "many-headed": "the many-headed multitude," "the many-headed mob," "the many-headed people," "the many-headed beast," "the many-headed monster." Many heads, but no brains. We abandon the building of the tower because we can only babble, not talk sense; we are the sailors in Plato's ship of fools (*Republic* 488), of whom "every one is of opinion that he has a right to steer, though he has never learned the art of navigation and cannot tell who taught him or when he learned, and will further assert that it cannot be taught." Therefore we "mutiny and take possession of the ship and make free with the stores; thus, eating and drinking, [we] proceed on [our] voyage in such a manner as might be expected." But however many we may be, we are all alike; we have no individual qualities or personal value. "Your *people*, Sir, is a great beast," said Hamilton. *Is*, not *are*. When you've seen one of us Yahoos, you've seen us all.

Swift's Yahoos, who first appeared in 1726, were not the first of their kind to appear in the Age of Reason. A year earlier, Vico's primitive giants had appeared: "destitute of any human custom and deprived of any human speech, and so in a state of wild animals . . . roving wild through the great forest of the earth . . . stupid, insensate, and horrible beasts" (*The New Science of Giambattista Vico*, trans. Thomas Goddard Bergin and Max Harold Fisch [Ithaca: Cornell University Press, 1968], sec. 62, 369, 374). Vico emphasized that human nature subsequently developed more humane forms; but his conception of our post-diluvian depravity was strongly influenced by Hobbes's less hopeful view, in *Leviathan* (1651), that our only real motive, even when we are apparently kind or generous, is and will continue to be nothing but self-interest: "Of the voluntary acts of every man, the object is some good to himself." Therefore, if one man does another a favor, or makes him a gift, it is "in hope to gain thereby friendship, or service from another, or from his friends; or in hope to gain the reputation of charity, or magnanimity; or to deliver his mind from the pain of compassion; or in hope of reward in Heaven" (ed. Oakeshott, pp. 86–87). "No man giveth, but with intention of good to himself; because gift is voluntary; and of all voluntary acts, the object is every man his own good" (p. 99). This being the case, "if any two men desire the same thing, which nevertheless they cannot both enjoy, they become enemies; and in the way to their end, which is principally their own conservation, and sometimes their delectation only, endeavour to destroy, or subdue one another" (p. 81). Therefore, as long as people "live without a common power to keep them all in awe," they are in a permanent state of warlike hostility "of every man, against every man . . . where every man is enemy to every man":

Chapter 4
The Beastly
People

> In such condition, there is no place for industry; because the fruit thereof is uncertain: and consequently no culture of the earth; no navigation, nor use of the commodities that may be imported by sea; no commodious building; no instruments of moving, and removing, such things as require much force; no knowledge of the face of the earth; no account of time; no arts; no letters; no society; and which is worst of all, continual fear, and danger of violent death; and the life of man, solitary, poor, nasty, brutish, and short. [P. 82.]

Thus human decency is possible only within the restraints imposed by an awe-inspiring power. Reason advises submission to such power; "the most part of men," however, "though they have the use of reasoning a little way," make as little use of it as children (p. 29); what actually causes them to live together peaceably, with laws of "justice, equity, modesty, mercy, and, in sum, doing to others, as we would be done to," is "the terror of some power, to cause them to be observed," since they are "contrary to our natural passions"; and "covenants, without the sword, are but words, and of no strength to secure a man at all" (p. 109). Therefore we submit to governments absolutely and unconditionally, like slaves or prisoners of war, our very lives being subject to their discretion or caprice; for "the commands of them that have the right to command, are not by their subjects to be censured, nor disputed. . . . And though of so unlimited a power, men may fancy many evil consequences, yet the consequences of the want of it, which is a perpetual war of every man against his neighbour, are much worse." Therefore subjects have only such liberty as the sovereign may choose to permit, and only so long as he may choose to permit it. "Nevertheless we are not to understand, that by such liberty, the sovereign power of life and death, is either abolished, or limited. For . . . nothing the sovereign representative [of God] can do to a subject, on what pretence soever, can properly be called injustice, or injury" (pp. 135–39). After developing this view of government in full detail, Hobbes concludes that it is correct because it is based "upon the known natural inclinations of mankind" (pp. 465–66).

That is to say, we are by nature unfit to govern ourselves, or even to make any decisions about our private lives except insofar as the sovereign power may choose for the time being to permit. We are by nature slaves, children, animals, who for our own good must submit to whatever sovereign power God may appoint to represent on earth his unknowable will and execute his unknowable purposes.

Vico's more humane view was largely unknown until our own time—Goethe heard of *The New Science* when he was in Italy, but his vague and fatuous brief comment in *Italian Journey* shows no knowledge or understanding of the text—and there is no reason to believe that Swift knew of it. Swift's Yahoos seem to be based rather on

Hobbes's conception of human nature; and their Houyhnhnm masters, being rational, are not human. This is the view that has generally prevailed, and continues to prevail, among conservatives.[2]

Nobody who believes that we are innately depraved can with any consistency believe in representative government. Though Hobbes's view was the official view throughout the brief period of the Restoration, the main current of seventeenth-century English life was against it; in 1688 the absolute monarchy he had celebrated was finally overthrown, and a kind of parliamentary government—by and for the rich, to be sure—was firmly established. A slight improvement lay in the fact that money is not absolutely impossible to acquire by our own efforts and is thus a little more accessible than aristocratic birth with its merely hereditary privileges. The new system of government made political power in England a little more generally accessible than it had been, and gradually, almost imperceptibly slowly, began to make English society somewhat freer: somewhat more amenable to living one's own life and developing one's own talents. Philosophic justification followed close behind events; it also encouraged, by justifying in advance, the emergence of later events. In 1699 Anthony Ashley Cooper, third earl of Shaftesbury, replied to Hobbes in *An Inquiry Concerning Virtue, or Merit*, and in 1711 gave the *Inquiry* wider circulation by reprinting it in Volume II of his collected chief works, *Characteristicks of Men, Manners, Opinions, Times*. (Note to the reader: I read the *Inquiry* in *Characteristicks* and took my notes on it several years ago in the British Museum; that was the first edition; the title page doesn't tell where it was published, or by whom; I am now writing this in the country north of Philadelphia, and it's raining, and I am not going to go into town to look up page numbers in a more easily accessible edition.)

[2] Adaline Glasheen writes, "Surely Swift's Yahoos are the Irish Roman Catholics."

Hobbes said our natural depravity is restrained, and we are compelled into an outward civility, by the fear of absolute and arbitrary power; Shaftesbury, a more humane man writing in a somewhat more liberal age, denied that all our natural impulses are bad; we have good impulses too, he said. "Vice and Virtue are found variously mix'd, and alternately prevalent in the several Characters of Mankind" (p. 38). It is "hard to pronounce of any Man, 'That he is *absolutely corrupt or vicious*' " (p. 39). This view he supports with six arguments:

1. Even an animal with nothing but hostility toward animals of his own kind would be unnatural and unimaginable, and so would a rational creature who enjoyed only vicious ideas and vicious behavior: " 'Tis impossible to suppose a mere sensible Creature originally so ill-constituted, and unnatural, as that from the moment he comes to be try'd by sensible Objects, he should have no one good Passion towards his Kind, no Foundation either of Pity, Love, Kindness, or social Affection. 'Tis full as impossible to conceive, that a rational Creature coming first to be try'd by rational Objects, and receiving into his Mind the Images or Representations of Justice, Generosity, Gratitude, or other Virtue, shou'd have no *Liking* of these, or *Dislike* of their Contrarys; but be found absolutely indifferent towards whatsoever is presented to him of this sort" (p. 43).

2. There is no absolute conflict between self-interest and "the Interest of *a Species,* or *common Nature.* " This is "demonstrated in the case of *natural Affection,* parental Kindness, Zeal for Posterity, Concern for the Propagation and Nurture of the Young, Love of Fellowship and Company, Compassion, mutual Succour, and the rest of this kind" (p. 78).

"According to his [Hobbes's] extraordinary Hypothesis, it must be taken for granted, 'That in the System of a Kind or Species, the Interest of *the private Nature* is directly opposite to that of *the common one;* the Interest of *Particulars* directly opposite to that of *the*

Publick in general.'—A strange Constitution! in which it must be confess'd there is much Disorder and Untowardness" (p. 80).

3. The fact that there are such feelings as pleasure and happiness indicates that there are good impulses. "There are few perhaps, who when they consider a Creature void of natural Affection, and wholly destitute of a communicative or social Principle, will suppose him, at the same time, either tolerably happy in himself, or as he stands abroad, with respect to his Fellow-Creatures or Kind. 'Tis generally thought, that such a Creature as this, feels but small Enjoyment in Life, and finds little satisfaction in the mere sensual Pleasures which remain with him, after the Loss of social Enjoyment; and all that can be call'd *Humanity* or *Good-Nature*" (p. 81). And just as absolute misery results from "this *total* Apostacy from all Candour, Equity, Trust, Sociableness, or Friendship," so proportionate degrees of misery result from various degrees of "this Depravity" (p. 82).

4. Intellectual pleasure is disinterested. Pleasure in mathematics, for example, "relates not in the least to any private Interest of the Creature, nor has for Object any Self-Good or Advantage of the private System. The Admiration, Joy, or Love turns wholly upon what is exteriour, and foreign to our-selves. And tho the reflected Joy or Pleasure, which arises from the notice of this Pleasure once perceiv'd, may be interpreted a *Self-Passion* or *interested Regard;* yet the original Satisfaction can be no other than what results from the Love of Truth, Proportion, Order, and Symmetry, in the Things without" (p. 104).

5. We enjoy the good of others, and thus participate in it. There is a natural pleasure in *"sharing Contentment and Delight with others,"* in observing their "Signs of Joy and Contentment" (pp. 107–08).

6. Even sensual pleasures are least satisfying in solitude. We like to eat and drink in company, to wear fine clothes among others who wear fine clothes, and to

give as well as receive pleasure in the sexual act. "This we may perceive by the perpetual Inconstancy, and Love of Change, so remarkable in those who have nothing communicative or friendly in their Pleasures" (pp. 126–29).

From these brief but representative extracts we can see the basic difference of method that led the two writers in such widely different directions: Hobbes proceeded by ratiocination, Shaftesbury by observation; in this respect Hobbes was a Platonist, proceeding from abstract premises to abstract conclusions, Shaftesbury an Aristotelian, proceeding from facts to conclusions based on facts; Hobbes a metaphysician, Shaftesbury an empiricist.

The traditional conservative hostility to science has usually been directed against the Aristotelian or experimental method much more than against the Platonic or ratiocinative method. Since Tertullian the attacks on particular logicians have seldom involved attacks on logic itself; and as far as I know there has never been a serious attack on mathematics itself. But conservatives are always afraid of undomesticated facts, especially those that don't fit into the received fundamentalism and those that show promise of improving the conditions of life for us common people. Barbey d'Aurevilly's attack on Diderot is quite typical:

It is impossible to write the history of the eighteenth century without running into the name and influence of Diderot, the indefatigable laborer at the *Encyclopédie,* who collected excrements, all the errors of the eighteenth century, and dumped them into that dung-cask, the *Encyclopédie*—but not to take them away!—in this respect inferior to the others who labor at that disgusting task. [Jules Barbey d'Aurevilly, *Goethe et Diderot. Iconoclaste* (Paris, E. Dentu, 1880), p. 147.]

That is of course not a serious argument, but it was the best Barbey could do. It is intellectually on a par with his dismissing all of Diderot's works because "He was of base extraction and always had bad manners. All his life he remained a petit bourgeois from Langres" (p. 131). A critic is reduced to scurrility and fatuity when he has neither facts nor wit to oppose to facts and wit.

Chapter 4
The Beastly
People

The collection and dissemination of facts through the *Encyclopédie,* and the witty presentation of them by the leading thinkers of the age—Diderot, d'Alembert, Voltaire, etc.—naturally alarmed those whose supra-social privileges depended on popular ignorance and inarticulacy. Then as now, the beneficiaries of corruption tried to keep the beastly people in the dark, so that their dissatisfaction would be vague, uninformed, unfocussed, groping, bewildered, naive, incoherent and inconsequent. The traditional conservative hostility to educating us common people is backed by the traditional conservative argument that we are ineducable; but the sneaky conservative machinations against the *Encyclopédie,* like similar efforts to suppress reports, articles, newspapers, magazines and books in other times and places, give the lie to that argument. Diderot predicted that the *Encyclopédie* would start an intellectual revolution, and it did. That's why eighteenth-century conservatives mutilated it as much as they could, and tried to suppress it entirely; that's why nineteenth-century conservatives, such as Barbey the fop, Gobineau the racist and Joseph de Maistre the defender of breaking on the wheel, asserted their delicate sensibilities against it; and that's why twentieth-century conservatives continue disingenuously to deplore it. (For an account of the mutilations and the efforts at suppression, see Douglas H. Gordon and Norman L. Torrey, *The Censoring of Diderot's Encyclopédie, and the Re-Established Text* [New York: Columbia University Press, 1947]; for two typical twentieth-century laments, see

Marshall McLuhan, *The Gutenberg Galaxy* [Toronto:
University of Toronto Press, 1962], and Hugh Kenner,
The Stoic Comedians [Boston: Beacon Press, 1962].)

Of course we have our creeps and cretins, as well as
our saints and sages; but few of us are any of these, and
most of us, as individuals, move on different levels at
different times, mentally and morally. Often we are
stupid, often we are weak, often we are cruel. The
populist view that we are the salt of the earth because
we are the people is as uncritical as the conservative
view that we are the scum of the earth because we are
the people. We are all different, from each other and
from ourselves, and no assumption that we are uniform
will work; for this reason, as well as from our personal
experience and observation, we know that Shaftesbury's
view of us is broader, clearer and more accurate than
Hobbes's. Most of us seem to mean well most of the
time.

Of course we don't always act well. We are often
deluded into acting badly in the belief that we are acting
well. The two chief classes of objects of delusion are
abstractions and idols. My friend and former colleague
Harold Lazarus says, "Never fall in love with an
abstraction." Bravo! And, I would add, never hate an
abstraction, never fear an abstraction, never pursue an
abstraction, never work for or against an abstraction. We
must always think of the particular effects of particular
acts on particular people.

But these cautionary refusals are hard for idolators;
and there are always idols. An idol is any institution that
we think of not as a collection of particular human
beings working together for a particular human purpose
or purposes but as a supra-human thing in itself, whose
purposes require us to regard human beings as
abstractions and treat them accordingly. Many
institutions tend to become idols.

The Whore of Babylon, idol and mother of
abominations, is always with us. She is any institution

that has become an end in itself—whether religious or secular, private or public, establishment or anti-establishment, local, regional, national or world-wide. She is always a saint who has lost her innocence but not her fervor; and she continues to attract some of her followers by the fervor with which she recalls to passersby the memory, or at least the tradition, of her innocence. We are naturally tempted to think of the courage with which she formerly resisted her oppressor, and to overlook her present wickedness; the temptation is especially strong in cases where the oppressor is still living, though she may now be collaborating with him in some respects or in all respects. The Building and Construction Trades Council, a confederation of labor unions, shares the racism of racist employers; the Holy Roman Empire was as imperialistic as the unholy Roman Empire; Soviet Russia is as repressive as Czarist Russia; and working-class fascist goons and hoodlums live by the same values as their contemptuous college-educated exploiters. When we respect the Whore of Babylon we are liable to have little or no respect for each other, or for ourselves. If we are not skeptical about her, we are liable to be cynical about each other, and about ourselves.

It is not fitting for us, the people, to deny our own intelligence, to play the pathetic, self-insulting role of John Q. Stupid, or to accept the notion that the people is a beast.

5

The Beastly Bourgeois;
or, The Discovery of America

In Robert Pinget's fantastic novel
Graal Flibuste (Paris; Les Editions de Minuit, 1956), we
visit briefly a little country named Dualia, where half the
men are farmers and half are sailors. The country is so
small that all the farms are in sight of the sea, and
therefore all the farmers wish they were sailors and all
the sailors wish they were farmers and nobody does
anything with any enthusiasm. The farmers of Dualia,
lacking enterprise, grow only the commonest staples; and
the sailors of Dualia, for the same reason, have not yet
discovered America.

It is not easy to discover America. Many Europeans—
not only those who follow dictators right and left, but
also those who peevishly sneer at the middle-class way of
life and plaintively sigh for the restoration of hereditary
classes—have not discovered America; and some
Americans have not discovered it either. The word
"bourgeois" in their mouths is a word of contempt. In
this the right and the left are as one.

On the right they look in the mirror and see—I don't know what they see, but presumably they don't see a person who earns a middle-class income and lives with more or less material comfort and more or less personal freedom in or near a town or city. In words if in nothing else, they dissociate themselves from the roots and sources of their own way of life: they sneer at money (though they use it); they sneer at representative government (though they benefit by it); they even sneer at science and its applications, which they call "gadgets" (though they wear glasses, drive cars, travel by plane, train and luxury liner, and communicate their disgust by radio, television, teletype, telephone, dictaphone and intercom).

The souls of the anti-bourgeois bourgeois of the right strike thoughtful or heroic attitudes. The religious and clothes-conscious Baudelaire raged against the political, economic and social "Americanization" of Europe:

> The world is coming to an end. . . . Mechanization will have so Americanized us, progress will have so dried up the spiritual part of us, that none of the bloodthirsty, sacrilegious or anti-natural dreams of utopians can be compared to its actual results. I ask every thinking man: Show me what remains of life. I believe it is useless to speak of or look for the remains of religion, since to take the trouble to deny God is now the only scandal in such matters. Property virtually disappeared with the repeal of the law of primogeniture; but the time will come when humanity, like a vengeful ogre, will tear the last bit from those who think they are the legitimate heirs of the revolutions. And even that will not be the supreme evil.
>
> The human imagination can conceive, without much difficulty, republics or other communal states that would be worthy of some glory, if they were directed by consecrated men, by certain aristocrats. But the universal ruin, or the universal progress—the

name matters little to me—will be manifested not particularly by political institutions, but by the degradation of hearts. . . . Then, the son will run away from home not at eighteen years of age but at twelve, emancipated by his gluttonous precocity; he will run away not in search of heroic adventures, not to set free a beauty held captive in a tower, not to immortalize a garret by sublime thoughts, but to establish a business, to get rich, to compete with his infamous papa—founder of and stockholder in a newspaper that spreads enlightenment. . . . Then, anything that resembles virtue—what am I saying?— anything that isn't ardor for Plutus will be regarded as a big joke. Justice—if in that fortunate epoch there is still something called justice—will outlaw citizens who can't make a fortune.—Thy wife, O Bourgeois! Thy chaste better half, whose legitimacy constitutes thy poetry—making pure unadulterated filthiness legal— vigilant and loving guardian of thy strongbox—will be nothing but the ideal perfection of the kept woman. Thy daughter, with infantile nubility, will dream in her cradle of selling herself for a million. And thou, O Bourgeois—even less a poet than now—wilt see nothing to change; thou wilt regret nothing. For there are elements in man that grow strong and flourish as others grow weak and dwindle, and, thanks to the progress of our age, nothing will remain inside thee but guts. [*Fusées* XV, in the Pléïade edition of the *Oeuvres Complètes* (Paris: Gallimard, 1961), pp. 1262–64.]

In a well-known rather prosy poem D. H. Lawrence went even farther. "How beastly the bourgeois is," he said:

Touch him, and you'll find he's all gone inside
Just like an old mushroom, all wormy inside, and
    hollow
under a smooth skin and an upright appearance.

These are fair and typical examples of the thought of those who yearn backward to a pre-bourgeois society. We should resist the temptation to dismiss such shriekers as merely bad-tempered, neurotic, pathetic and foolish: there are too many of them for that, and they write too well. They are a real danger. With comparable measure, objectivity and urbanity, Ortega y Gasset complained that unemployment had so decreased that it was almost impossible to find good servants, and when you did find them you had to guard your tongue because they wanted to be spoken to politely; Aldous Huxley said ordinary people were only spoiled by such luxuries as steam heat, running water, armchairs, etc., which should be reserved for the intelligent—whom he identified with those who had inherited good libraries and could afford to send their children to expensive private schools: he recommended the abolition of public education and the popularization of chemically induced cheap brainless instant mysticism—i.e., of hallucinogenic drugs. D. H. Lawrence said workers should wear red pants and dance in the sun and stop bothering their weak heads about such abstractions as wages and working conditions. He wanted Lady Ottoline Morrell to finance a utopian community of natural lords and ladies, including him, ruled by a natural king and queen and waited on by natural servants—who in such free time as they might be granted would presumably wear red pants and dance in the sun and grin picturesquely and say, "Yassuh, boss!" C. S. Lewis at Oxford lamented that so many earnest plebeians were getting into the universities, as Santayana at Harvard before him had lamented that Jews were getting in; and T. S. Eliot explicitly rejected the principle of equality of opportunity.

A number of living writers continue to sing the old song. Jacques Barzun, in *The House of Intellect* (New York: Harper, 1959), says intellect is not necessarily a keen mind but rather a lifelong habituation to good literature, good music, etc.—a habituation by which alone high culture can be perpetuated; for him, high culture is less an individual attainment than a family habit, custom or tradition; he therefore frankly prefers gentle mediocrities sprung from families with good libraries—such presumably as Thomas Bailey Aldrich, George Edward Woodberry, Marthe Bibesco and J. Donald Adams—to upstart geniuses sprung from families with few or no books—such presumably as Walt Whitman, Mark Twain, Thorstein Veblen, Kant, Dickens and Joyce. The attitude of proprietary exclusiveness is carried beyond Professor Barzun's politic reserve by Hugh Kenner in *The Stoic Comedians* and by Marshall McLuhan (the admen's guru) in *The Gutenberg Galaxy.* Both these well-read men deplore the invention of printing, the spread of literacy and the increasing availability of all kinds of information to all kinds of people; they prefer the values of the middle ages to those of the Enlightenment. That is to say, they would like to see a small and exclusively literate leisure class (though most of the medieval aristocrats, throughout most of the period, were illiterate), a large humble picturesque illiterate peasantry and servant class, and the minimum possible number of intelligent burghers in between. Which is to say the minimum possible number of unpicturesque bourgeois: self-respecting people who earn middle-class incomes and live with more or less material comfort and more or less personal freedom (much more now than then) in or near a town or city: people who have discovered America.

The fact that such views have a certain currency need not distress us unduly at the moment. Their influence here and now is less than it has been at most times in most places. But we should continually counteract them. Fascist regimes do in fact restore, insofar as possible, the old pre-bourgeois system of class privileges; it is no accident that they always have the support of most of the big rich and most of the surviving aristocrats; and those who back the American government's invariable support of such regimes in other countries would undoubtedly welcome one here if they thought they could get away with it. The danger they represent should never be overlooked or underestimated. Perhaps the most insidious danger at the moment is a tendency that would let them get away with it: a tendency for such attacks from the right to be wittingly or unwittingly reinforced by large numbers of sincere or insincere leftists, who also want us to consider classes and categories more important than individuals—i.e., to prejudge people as "class enemies" or "class allies" rather than to judge them on the basis of their behavior as individuals—and who want to blunt and stultify our intelligence by leveling down instead of "equalizing upward."

I owe the phrase "equalizing upward" to my friend the brilliant painter Morris Blackburn, who struggles in his art classes, as I struggle in my English classes, to counteract the widespread notion that the idea is everything and the execution nothing, that form and content have nothing to do with each other, that technique serves no purpose, at least no honest purpose, and that concern with technique militates against freedom of expression. Given all these premises, it is easy enough to conclude—and many students do conclude—that skill in any kind of artistic performance (unlike skill in sports) is mere vanity and dishonesty, and hence that an unskillful performance is better, morally and artistically. This belief involves the unexamined corollary that content is independent of and unaffected by form. So that when students of mine write such sentences as "We built a fire in the old fashion wooden stove," "The court system is the main protest of the novel, however Dickens is not a utopian panacreas for all the ills of socalled society," "Emma Bovary was an incurable romantic who yearned to be carried away by a knight in shinny armor and old castles," and "Nabokov seemed to style his novels around the adolescent small-breasted type of girl," I find it difficult to make them see that the content of a sentence is what its words actually say, not what some other words might say, and I usually find it impossible to make them see that form is either controlled and deliberate self-expression or uncontrolled and inadvertent self-revelation—that the style is the mind, that the style increasingly becomes the mind, and that we create ourselves accordingly. We would not tolerate such vague gropings and mere approximations on the part of a brain surgeon, a basketball player or an airplane pilot, but we fear to be precise in our own thinking about human problems, lest we displease Lady Ottoline. Semiliteracy is the opium of the people.

I doubt that many of us would be delighted if we paid admission to hear a violinist who couldn't even play in tune—and whose ear didn't tell him he was out of tune —on the basis that intention is performance. But if the present tendency in education continues—the tendency to call incompetence creativity—even that may come to pass. We already buy paintings and sculptures whose only virtue is their intention, and poems, plays and novels written with comparable skill. There are people who think all you have to do to be Jesus Christ is let your hair and beard grow and all you have to do to be the Blessed Virgin Mary is have a baby whose father is God knows who and all you have to do to be Sappho or Shakespeare is have a homosexual hangup and a ball-point pen and all you have to do to be James Joyce is write like John Lennon.

Such intellectual slackness makes us easy prey for sincere-talking salesmen of easy solutions to hard problems, and willing accomplices in our own bamboozlement by those who would have us leave all hard problems to Lady Ottoline. It is disastrously easy to yield to the seductiveness of the Grand Inquisitor's "Miracle, Mystery, and Authority," or Carlyle's "Work, Wonder, and Worship," or Vichy France's "Work,

Family, Country," or the U.S. Defense Department's "Duty, Honor, Country," to say nothing of Nazi Germany's formulation of the proper concerns of women: "Children, Kitchen, Church." All these magic incantations militate against thought. They all express a view of us common people as children or dull clunks to be kept busy and not consulted; and if we are permitted and thereby encouraged to see no difference between

"wood" and "wooden," and not to see that the statement "The court system is the main protest of the novel" inadvertently reveals blurred thinking, we conform ourselves to that view of us, and create ourselves in that image. We make ourselves incoherent. We make ourselves unable to think clearly.

When we reduce ourselves to that state we become susceptible to the clichés floating in the air—and clichés are infectious. One of the most virulent is the notion that we of the middle class—we bourgeois—are not interested in anything but (1) money and (2) the things it can buy: (a) possessions and (b) social status. Baudelaire's attacks were quite typical of those of furious rightists; those of furious leftists are remarkably similar. Listen, for example, to this representative excerpt from a pamphlet by two leftist bourgeois—a philosopher with a D. Phil. dissertation on the philosophy of Epicurus, named Karl Marx, and a textile manufacturer with authoritarian manners, named Friedrich Engels—*The Communist Manifesto:*

> The bourgeoisie has stripped of its halo every occupation hitherto honored and looked up to with reverent awe. It has converted the physician, the lawyer, the priest, the poet, the man of science, into its paid wage-laborers.
>
> The bourgeoisie has torn from the family its sentimental veil, and has reduced the family relation to a mere money relation.

Can your relationship with your family be expressed in terms of money? And look around you. Do these gross caricatures have any recognizable resemblance to you or any of your friends? Of course there are such people: we run into them here and there, now and then, and as I write they are in charge of the executive branch of the U.S. government; but they are in trouble with us because they misrepresent us. In choosing or accepting them as our leaders we were deceived; sooner or later we will correct our mistake and refuse to follow them any farther. A society made up of such people would have no more stability than Hobbes's state of nature. They are grotesques, not normal social beings.

Neither Baudelaire's nor Marx's and Engels' view of us bourgeois can be taken seriously. But there are calmer derogations that must be taken seriously. Chaucer made fun of us, Shakespeare made fun of us, Molière made fun of us, most of the great novelists, poets and playwrights have regarded us with various degrees and combinations of amusement, pity, distaste, contempt and horror.

Why?

All their objections can be summed up in three principal objections: (1) that getting and spending, we lay waste our powers; (2) that we have no taste or manners; (3) that we have no sense of personal honor.

To the extent that these objections are leveled not at particular acts of individuals but at all of us as a class, and at our way of life in vague generality, they have no more validity than other prejudices. But they *are* leveled at all of us as a class; they *are* leveled at our way of life in vague generality; and most of the objectors are themselves bourgeois. For the standards of social value evolve much more slowly than the facts of social organization; therefore the risen middle class continues to live to a large extent by the metaphors and rituals of the ancient and medieval leisure classes, replacing them only slowly and partially with its own. The middle class is unique among classes in having a bad conscience about its own values. Pardon me—you see how easy it is to slip into the featureless generalizations of scholastic realism—I mean the middle class is unique among classes in producing a considerable number of thoughtful men and women who have a bad conscience about the prevailing values of the society their class has made. Some turn romantically backward to the older values; some turn angrily away to values based on newer facts and not yet socially established.

The success of the ancient Romans in governing their heterogeneous empire was due in part to their using native administrators and civil servants; and the early medieval Western church, in its task of evangelizing the heathen, found it essential to set up local churches staffed by natives. But the work of a priest or bishop, unlike that of a political boss, required some intellectual training; therefore the church set up monastic schools, whose work served to plant a few seeds of the Roman intellectual culture among the Western barbarians—even though many of the clergy were in fact disastrously ignorant, and even though the church seems to have burned more books than it preserved. From those few seeds sprang not only the scholastic culture of the middle ages but also the intellectual roots of the Reformation that destroyed it from within and the Renaissance philosophy that succeeded it. And of course the church and the governing class, though they had their differences and rivalries, usually worked together.[1]

---

[1] Adaline Glasheen writes, "Words like 'Reformation' look very different in Ireland, where to the delectation of people like Elizabeth and Raleigh and Spenser the Reformed went casting about like Alva in the Netherlands or Hitler in Belsen. For my new book [a Third Census of *Finnegans Wake*] I lately read Spenser's *View of Ireland,* as pretty a little genocidal tract as you'd want to read in a month of Sundays. (It's another shining example of how well the wicked can sometimes write.) And the *View* was a favorite work of Milton's, who pressed it on Cromwell, who exults in his massacre of Papist babies in Drogheda. So poets DO make things happen, as Pound's writings inspired that

Thus, whatever home-made values the mass of people may have lived by in their daily living, the official values of Western Europe since the conversion of the Emperor Constantine—the values promulgated in churches, courts and schools—have been the values of a Christianized royalty and aristocracy; and now that government has generally passed into the hands of a middle class whose working values are largely secular, we still profess a ritual or ceremonial allegiance to the values of Christianized royalty and aristocracy.

These values are said to be of a spiritual nature and to involve a sense of social responsibility unknown to us materialistic and self-seeking bourgeois. The historian Vico, the poet Nietzsche and the ironist Veblen have all defined them in terms of temperament.

Vico, in *The New Science* (trans. Thomas Goddard Bergin and Max Harold Fisch [Ithaca: Cornell University Press, 1968]), tells in much detail how the priest-kings who organized and led the first human societies, and the heroes or feudal aristocrats who succeeded them, ruled by personal force and arbitrariness with the backing of Divine Providence. In order to tame and control the human race, who after the flood had become mere animals (sec. 62, 172, 369–73), the priest-kings and heroes were by nature "boorish, crude, harsh, wild, proud, and obstinate in their resolves" (sec. 708), and their laws and established customs were "crude, inhuman, cruel, uncivilized and monstrous" (sec. 102). When the people overthrew them and established "popular commonwealths," the laws and customs became more humane (sec. 1022–26). (For more on Vico's view of history, see my article "Where Terms Begin," in *A Conceptual Guide to Finnegans Wake*, ed. Michael H. Begnal and Fritz Senn [University Park, Pa.: Penn State University Press, 1974], pp. 1–17.)

dreadful American Nazi Kasper to interfere with school desegregation in the South."

Nietzsche, in *The Genealogy of Morals* (trans. Francis Golffing trans. [Garden City, N.Y.: Doubleday Anchor Books, 1956]), identifies psychological health with domination, and sickness with submission; he cannot conceive any honest human relationship but that of domination and submission; he sees religion as merely a fraudulent substitute for personal strength of arm, a contemptible means by which the clever sick dominate the stupid sick; to the extent that the strong use it (as they use political trickery) as a substitute for personal strength, they behave unworthily—worthy behavior for the strong consisting not in soothing or cajoling or comforting the slaves into submission but in beating them into submission, making them feel not less but more pain in their lot, while at the same time competing with other strong enslavers to enslave each other. Competition is the admirable virtue of the strong, cooperation the contemptible virtue of the weak:

Chapter 5
The Beastly
Bourgeois; or,
The Discovery
of America

> Whenever the former join forces, it is done solely in view of some concerted aggressive action, some gratification of the will to power, and invariably against the resistance of individual consciences. . . . The entire course of history bears out the fact that every oligarchy conceals a desire for tyranny. Every oligarchy vibrates with the tension which each individual member must maintain in order to master that desire. [P. 273.]

The danger in using religion instead of brute strength as a means of keeping the slaves submissive is that the masters themselves may come to believe its promises, and so be psychologically corrupted (pp. 276–80).

But Nietzsche knows no economics or sociology. He despises such dismal knowledge. He is not concerned with commonplace facts. He overlooks them. Veblen, a cooler and much more rigorous thinker, recalls our distracted attention to them. In *The Theory of the Leisure*

Class (New York: Modern Library, no date), he makes a distinction, which Nietzsche does not make, between devout observances and ethical behavior. Neither implies the other, of course; and, as Veblen observes,

> In the older communities of the European culture, the hereditary leisure class, together with the mass of the indigent population, are given to devout observances in an appreciably higher degree than the average of the industrious middle class, wherever a considerable class of the latter character exists. [P. 320.]

This is because the middle class, subject to "the point of view which the modern industrial life inculcates," habitually regards phenomena in terms of their practical causes and effects (p. 319), whereas the hereditary leisure class habitually regards them in terms of their ceremonial value, i.e., their value as symbols of status (p. 314), and the indigent classes "ordinarily stand in such a relation of dependence or subservience to their pecuniary superiors as materially to retard their emancipation from habits of thought proper to the régime of status" (p. 319)—i.e., from considering phenomena chiefly in terms of their ceremonial or animistic significance.

In the modern world the hereditary leisure class blends in with the upper bourgeoisie, and the traditional distinctions between them are blurred; the leisure class is found in its purest form not in the modern world but "at the higher stages of the barbarian culture"—e.g., "in feudal Europe or feudal Japan" or "Brahmin India" (p. 1); its members "are by custom exempt or excluded from industrial occupations, and are reserved for employments to which a degree of honour attaches. . . . These non-industrial upper-class occupations may be roughly comprised under government, warfare, religious observances, and sports" (pp. 1–2). These occupations all involve manifestations of personal prowess toward, or personal influence on or over, animals, human beings, or personified forces of nature; they therefore have more emotional appeal than mere industry, however skillful, and are therefore regarded in the popular apprehension as spiritually superior: the man who exercises or represents power is more highly regarded than the man or woman who doesn't; the man who takes is more highly regarded than the man or woman who makes; the warrior's force is more highly regarded than the artisan's or artist's skill; the hunter has a natural right, by virtue of his personal superiority, to ride over and trample down the farmer's vegetables, especially if he hunts not from necessity but for sport. And the habits of thought proper to the barbarian leisure-class occupations persist, with only tactical modifications, in the modern world:

> The relation of the leisure (that is, propertied non-industrial) class to the economic process is a pecuniary relation—a relation of acquisition, not of production; of exploitation, not of serviceability. . . . The conventions of the business world have grown up under the selective surveillance of this principle of predation or parasitism. They are conventions of ownership; derivatives, more or less remote, of the ancient predatory culture. [P. 209.]

That is to say, the top management of modern business is concerned less with production than with finance—with the manipulation of shares of ownership and the increase of capital: capital whose basic purpose is not to increase production but to acquire more property—i.e., more capital, more money. Therefore the top salaries, bonuses, stock options, expense accounts and other financial rewards of modern business go not to its engineers, chemists and other production people but to its money managers. Moreover, when in the course of corporate events the interest of the corporation conflicts with the private interest of its president or board chairman, the interest of the corporation is sacrificed. E.g., it may pay a higher price for an inferior piece of equipment because its board chairman sells that equipment; or it may lose money for a period, in order to enable its president to sell his shares of stock at the current high price and buy them back at the later low price. For more exciting details, don't miss Veblen's *The Theory of Business Enterprise*, a book that in 1903 predicted the coming of fascism.

But the traditional conception of the bourgeoisie is of a class of mere industrious drudging unimaginative unspiritual contemptible humble producers and distributors of goods and services: guildsmen, small manufacturers, merchants, apothecaries, doctors, lawyers, accountants, notaries. The aristocratic contempt of the leisure class for the bourgeoisie was taken over, not entirely but to an unduly large extent, by Marx and Engels, who recognized the great improvements brought about by the bourgeois revolutions of 1688, 1776 and 1789 but underestimated and undervalued the continuing basic liberalism of the bourgeoisie, notwithstanding all relapses and retreats, and wanted to replace it with something very like the old illiberal autocracy, only this time not in the hands of royalty or aristocrats but in the hands of workers' committees. It did not occur to them that censorship and repression are always bad, no matter who exercises them; or that the state will never wither away; or that the means tend to become the end.

Thus the acquisitive accuse us of being acquisitive, the unmannerly accuse us of being unmannerly, the irresponsible accuse us of being irresponsible, the repressive accuse us of being repressive. And from right and left we are attacked by literary intellectuals, themselves bourgeois, who should know better. The arts, the letters, the humanities, the amenities, are of course not necessities of life; they are in the nature of luxuries.

Luxuries, being associated primarily with the life of the leisure class, have more ceremonial value than necessities —a jeweler or an art dealer is not quite so contemptible a bourgeois as an equally wealthy coal or lumber dealer —because luxuries represent what Veblen called "conspicuous consumption," an evidence of prowess, exploit, spiritual superiority, status (pp. 68–101); for the same reason, the cultivation of the arts, the letters, etc.,

is one way of representing "conspicuous leisure" (pp. 35–67, 363–400)—an economic ability to spend time cultivating sensibilities that have nothing to do with getting the necessities of life. There are those who say we common people have no capacity for such refinements of perception, and there are those who say we should not develop them because they are of no use or value to the working class; the former call themselves conservative, the latter call themselves radical. They are both wrong. They are both reactionary. They both distrust free human minds. No matter what they call themselves, they have not discovered America.

6

The Noble Savage;
or, Backing Away from Nature

Politics, like nature, often imitates bad art; and each lends its countenance to the other's excesses.

Nature has a weakness for nineteenth-century overemphasis and noise. Every storm at sea is an idiotically enthusiastic performance of the overture to *The Flying Dutchman;* and what could be in worse taste than an earthquake, a landslide, a volcanic eruption, a tidal wave, or a tornado? Nature lacks proportion, decorum, decency, manners.

So does politics. The charge of the light brigade was a corny dramatization of Tennyson's corny poem; wars are made by people who are not amused but thrilled by the "1812 Overture" and "Off we go, into the wild blue yonder"; political scandals are made by tough-talking permanent adolescents who think in the uncivilized gut-language of spy novels, gangster movies and TV commercials, and act accordingly; and depressions are made by people addicted to the same cheap dreams, in their roles as rodeo-managers of the economy: though the rodeo is rigged, they see nothing wrong with that, they take it as a matter of course, and urge us to trust "natural forces." I quote.

Our troubles are due less to the policies of evil men in high places than to the policies of corny men in high places, doing what comes naturally. They don't lack moral zeal, these prayer-breakfast promoters and enemies of nuance; they lack style, grace, wit, and a civilized sense of the oafish. Beware the noble savage. His tasteless innocence could do us in. If there is any hope for us, it is the hope that we can find among ourselves, and persuade to stand forth, leaders with some tincture or taint of civilization.

Neither Rousseau nor Dryden nor Las Casas invented the noble savage, nor did any of the seven types of pastoral poets, nor did any of our current apostles of ignorance, though they think they did. God invented him, or rather them, and named them Adam and Eve: two innocents who became corrupted by the artificialities of civilization: by knowledge and the desire for knowledge. As soon as their eyes were opened, they were no longer in Paradise. ("Paradise," my fellow sinners, is a Persian word meaning garden.) Or perhaps —it doesn't matter, the result is the same either way— they saw that what they had thought was a garden was really a wilderness. But whichever way it was, we, their children, have longed ever since to return to that Paradise or relapse into that sweet delusion, eating lotus and riding like Peer Gynt's trolls on pigs that we take for horses—we have dramatized our longing in many myths and metaphors.

Compare the look of mindless sensuality on the face of Botticelli's just-born Venus with the look of depraved intelligence on the face of Caravaggio's adolescent Bacchus. She is unfallen Eve in Paradise; he is fallen Adam in the civilized world: his face is alive with humorous intelligence—he understands everything, for

Chapter 6
The Noble
Savage;
or, Backing
Away from
Nature

better and for worse—but he is soft, lazy, slightly drunk, no longer amoral but immoral; and my wife reminds me that he doesn't know whether he's a boy or a girl. These two—the noble savage, innocent of all knowledge and therefore good, and the civilized human being, depraved *because* civilized—are two metaphorical figures with which we delude ourselves.

Our delusion involves three errors: (1) that innocence and goodness are identical, (2) that nature is necessarily good, and (3) that civilization is necessarily bad. These errors affect everything from our aesthetics to our educational system to our voting laws, which still, after all reapportionments, discriminate against city-dwellers.

Innocence is neither good nor bad. A new-born infant is neither good nor bad. He or she is morally non-existent. I don't say morally neutral—neutrality, the attitude of the angels who landed in limbo, is something altogether different. We don't say that a tree or a bee is morally neutral, for example, because we know that trees and bees don't make moral choices and that the terms "moral," "immoral" and "neutral" simply don't apply to them, any more than they would apply to a pencil sharpener; but somehow we assume that they do apply to all human beings, including those just born, who we assume do have a moral nature even though they have no experience. Even in our secular age many people believe that babies are born depraved and must have their depravity washed away as soon as possible, and others believe that babies are born good and must be protected insofar as possible from the corrupting influences of civilization. But infant innocence is the innocence of a tree or a bee, which is neither morally good nor morally bad nor morally neutral. We develop our moral nature gradually, by the choices we make in action.

The belief that nature is good and artifice is bad is largely responsible for the seriousness with which people who should know better take the plays of Sam Shepard or the alleged sculptures of people whose sculpting consists of filling a room with smoke or turning on the water in the sink or hanging a sheet in a tree or leaning a board against a wall. And why else would so many people who should know better give serious attention to such kitschy imitations of folk music as those of Grand Ole Opry Inc. and rock groups managed from offices in London and New York? With amplifiers and electronic instruments, these painstakingly unkempt and self-consciously illiterate bards hard-sell their macrobiotic love, their psychedelic mind-mashing and their contemptuous pseudo-populism. In their naive belief that the mind—the distinctively human element that distinguishes us from the other animals—is an unnatural and unworthy late superaddition that only makes us sick, these and other commercially sick souls try to lead us back en masse—en mentally helpless hard-buying masse—to mindless nature. They think nature is a sucker with money to spend. They think all of civilization is as corrupt as they are.

Chapter 6
The Noble
Savage;
or, Backing
Away from
Nature

Of course I know our civilization is bad in many ways. When my wife and I drive into Philadelphia we can smell some of them. To us who live on a green subrural hillside the air of Philadelphia smells noticeably of gasoline and diesel oil fumes; so does the air of New York; so does the air of Washington; so, doubtless, does the air of every other city of any size; when on our way to or from the Philadelphia airport we pass through the small city of Conshohocken, where tires are made, we close our windows against the stink of sulphur fumes; and near the airport we cross a high bridge over acres of smoking and flaring oil refineries, a hell of dirt and drear. Most industries create hells of dirt and drear; and many, such as strip mining and steel-making, create hells dreary enough to satisfy the most religious.

Still, city life is not all hell, not always hell, not necessarily hell. We lived in New York for some fifteen years, and enjoyed it very much; and though when we go back we are dismayed to see that Washington Square, for example, formerly a place for lovers, chess players, roller skaters, and mothers airing their babies, is now full of miserable prostitutes, pimps and dope pushers, and that the city generally seems dirtier, smokier, smoggier and smellier than it used to be—still, we have friends who live there by choice and enjoy it almost as much as we did. True, they are all fairly well off, so that hell isn't just outside their doors—or inside either. But life is hell for the poor in the suburbs too, and even more so in the country. There is no slum quite so slummy as a rural slum. The only thing worse than living in a rural slum would be living in a state of nature.

No human being lives in a state of nature. Even the most primitive societies—those that explorers in helicopters discover for educational TV—have their physical and psychological safeguards against nature, their improvements over nature. Dugout canoes don't occur in nature; arrows don't occur in nature; explanations of nature, be they scientific or mythic or mystical, don't occur in nature. Everything that is distinctively human is artificial. To give up everything but what occurs in nature would be to give up being human. Even the nature nuts know this. Ask a person who wants to go back to nature how far back he wants to go, and you'll find that he personally doesn't want to go back very far at all, because his nature doesn't permit him to. He does, to be sure, want to live a life of mere instinct and unmediated impulse; but he wants to take with him into that paradise, if not a book, at least a pack of Tarot cards or an astrological chart. And a flashlight. And an axe. And a bedroll. Etc., etc.—it's quite a shopping list, and the more he actually knows about life under the stars the longer it is. Army-Navy store, here he comes! Abercrombie & Fitch, here he comes! At the very least, in most cases, he doesn't want to go out there naked—*au naturel.*

And of course he doesn't want to go just any old where in nature. He will choose his spot with some care. That is to say, he won't even consider most of the spots —because most of nature isn't fit for human habitation. Nature isn't all Corot, Constable, Pissarro, Morisot or Sisley, much less Arcady, Green Mansions, Maxfield Parrish, Bali Hai, or the nature department of Disneyland. Nature is underbrush. Nature is thorns. Nature is swamps, deserts, scorpions, snakes, rats, mosquitoes, hornets and blowflies. And of course nature is hurricanes, tornadoes, blizzards, earthquakes, floods, and other natural phenomena that insurance companies call acts of God. Nature is laissez-faire. Nature destroys nature. So when anybody says he wants to go back to nature, I wonder if he knows what he is saying.

Chapter 6
The Noble
Savage;
or, Backing
Away from
Nature

Most writers, even most romantic writers, know better. In literature nature is usually inhabited not by noble savages but by civilized people, who whether shipwrecked or exiled or voluntarily retired live as comfortably as they can: Robinson Crusoe or the Swiss Family Robinson, who in both cases had a good supply of tools, instruments and weapons, and who never gave up hope of returning to civilization; or Robin Hood, who lived in constant contact with civilization and took what he wanted from it; or Mr. Wilson and family in *Joseph Andrews,* who lived quietly in the country, raising their own vegetables and making their own ale, on the proceeds of an invested fortune, which though not large enabled them to be charitable to their neighbors and to work in their garden for reasons of health and enjoyment rather than of necessity; or Emile and his friend Sophy, whom Rousseau explicitly called abstractions, and whose education in the free sincerity of nature he contrived and controlled with rigorous artificiality.

Rousseau himself spent most of his life reading and writing, in cities that were centers of intellectual activity or in the country among bluestockings and *philosophes,* not in agronomic activity or sporting with Amaryllis in the shade. In this he was like most writers, however romantic. Too much fresh air is bad for the style. Wordsworth was outdoors when he saw those daffodils, but tranquilly indoors when he wrote about them. From Theocritus, Bion and Moschus, who wrote not for working shepherds or neatherds but for Alexandrian or Syracusan aesthetes (which is not by any means to say they were bad poets), through Virgil, the very model of a court poet (which is not by any means to say he was a bad poet), through their classically educated Renaissance imitators and Romantic adapters, down to, oh, say down to Tolstoy, with two exceptions those who recommended living close to nature either spent most of their lives in cities or lived in the country surrounded by books and attended by servants.

The two exceptions were Burns and Hogg, two dirt farmers. Burns was not primarily a nature poet, and the few poems in which he celebrated simple rural living— e.g., "The Cotter's Saturday Night"—were belied by his father's experience and his own, which apparently gave him a heart condition; in any case, primarily because of the condition of his purse, he wound up not a farmer but a tax collector. Hogg's sweet lyrics, which appealed to city-dwellers and gentleman farmers, served chiefly to bring him, after he had failed as a practicing farmer, the gift of a tenanted farm where he could be the gentleman.[1] So far as I know, there are no examples of writers who succeeded in living by their toil with the soil. Carlyle? No. He stayed indoors at Craigenputtock, writing. Jean Giono? No. That propagandist for oxen as against tractors moved to the country only after he had

[1] Robert M. Adams, in his introduction to the Norton Library edition of Hogg's *The Private Memoirs and Confessions of a Justified Sinner,* puts it succinctly: "But what he made on books, he lost on farms, and after some years of unsuccessful scrabbling he went to Edinburgh." There he wrote the sweet lyrics, as Samuel Woodworth wrote "The Old Oaken Bucket" in New York City.

made a lot of money as a writer—that celebrant of peasant life never lived it. Robert Frost? No. He never made a living altogether by farming. The two chief uses he made of the farm he was pressured into accepting were to sell it—which he did as soon as he was permitted to—and to write about it. In "Two Tramps in Mudtime" he says farm work is his avocation, not his vocation; in "I'm going out . . ." he goes out to clean the pasture spring for pleasure, promising his wife that he won't be gone long and inviting her to share the pleasure with him. That is not the attitude of a pro.

Chapter 6
The Noble
Savage;
or, Backing
Away from
Nature

Please don't anybody mention Thoreau. In Arcadia, when he was there, he didn't see any hammering stone. I like his occasional wit, as here; but it tends to be allusive, as here, not natural; and I am not uplifted by the heavy censorious preaching that is his much more usual tone. He went part way back to nature now and then by way of surcease and vacation: a week on the Concord and Merrimack rivers, ten days in Quebec, several trips to the Maine woods and to Cape Cod, and the two wonderful years at Walden pond—where he had tools, books, pens, ink, paper, and visiting Concord intellectuals. And a Harvard education, my wife reminds me. Few men have been more smug. He bought most of his food in town—the most expensive item being rice produced by coolie labor in the land of Buddha or by slave labor in the land of Calhoun and brought to him by railroads, whose existence he deplored—and paid for it by working in town. He recognized, if only by his acts, that life in a state of nature was not for him.

What is valuable in Thoreau is not his naturizing but his respect for the inner life, including quite explicitly the intellect—for the cultivation of which he said society should afford more leisure than it does—and his contempt for the life of domination and submission. In both these respects he is far superior to our modern naturizers, who from Tolstoy onward have tended to be anti-intellectuals, and from Nietzsche onward anti-democrats.

These starting points are of course arbitrary, but no more so than any others we might choose, and they are convenient because they are far back enough to give us some background but not so far back as to change the subject on us. I take it that the readers of this book know that Tolstoy didn't invent anti-intellectualism, or Nietzsche authoritarianism, and that the two diseases have usually gone together.

What makes Tolstoy and Nietzsche especially convenient for our purpose is that they were both naturizers. I don't mean that Nietzsche went herborizing like Rousseau, much less that he went swinging a scythe like Tolstoy; I mean that his influence has survived the defeat of the Nazis and is still with us in the continuing influence of D. H. Lawrence, Yeats, St. Exupéry, Gide, Giono, and other writers who have propagated the notion that thought is a poor substitute for instinct and impulse. This notion, together with Tolstoy's theory of art and the romantic appeal of Kostya Levin in *Anna Karenina*, has lent itself in our time to the purposes of authoritarians, who would govern through conditioned reflexes rather than through the uncoerced intelligence of the governed.

103
The Noble
Savage;
or, Backing
Away from
Nature

For the pathetic fallacy operates in political theory as well as in poetry. Nature is neither kind nor cruel, neither liberal nor conservative, neither democratic nor aristocratic, neither parliamentarian nor authoritarian; but the advocates and opponents of every political theory have always based their claims on nature, and have always tried to justify them by unjustifiable analogies between human and non-human nature. That old Tory Dr. Johnson thought it was *unnatural* for women to write.

Tolstoy's Rousseauian notion that education in the arts perverts our natural good taste and throws off our instinctive right judgment—i.e., that any "uncorrupted" peasant is a better judge of painting than any art historian, or that any illiterate Lapland Eskimo is a better judge of literature than any lifelong student of literature

—led him to unorthodox conclusions that he didn't evade: that *Hamlet* is artistically worthless, that Beethoven's sonata Opus 101 is inferior to any Hungarian folk dance or Russian folk song chosen at random, that the novels of Zola and Huysmans are inferior to a story about an Easter cake in a children's magazine, etc. (*What is Art?*, ch. 14). He wallowed in the affective fallacy because he valued feeling above thought, because he regarded kind, social feelings as natural, and unkind, aggressive feelings as unnatural, and because he associated thought with unnatural feeling or with no feeling: with immorality, hypocrisy, and snobbery. But there is no snob like an affective snob, who considers his own feelings purer and more natural than others'. The conviction of our own affective purity justifies all our sins, even those of the most conventional social snobbery. V. Veresayev reports a conversation between his friend "G." and a peasant near Tolstoy's estate:

*Chapter 6
The Noble
Savage;
or, Backing
Away from
Nature*

"Do you see Tolstoy?"

"Oh yes, ever so often."

"Well, what is he like?"

"Not bad, a serious old man. If you meet him on the road he will talk to you; then it's as if he put out his hand to keep you away: 'Don't get too near, I am a Count.' "

Veresayev approached Tolstoy as a pilgrim, full of love, reverence, awe and trepidation—and found him cold and disagreeable: " 'Ah, yes, political freedom,' said Tolstoy, waving his hand contemptuously, 'it is neither necessary nor important. What *is* important, is moral perfection and love, these, and not freedom, create kindliness among men" (V. Veresayev, "A Day with Tolstoy," in Cyril Connolly's anthology *The Golden Horizon* [New York: University Books, 1955], pp. 303, 307). We have heard it from Allen Tate, John Crowe Ransom and Donald Davidson, defenders of slavery; from Billy Graham, Norman Vincent Peale and Richard Nixon, defenders of knavery. Tolstoy's doctrine of non-resistance to evil consists perfectly with his doctrine that nature reflects the divine goodness and justice. It was a doctrine that enabled him to put on a peasant blouse and go barefooted and still be a Count.[2]

But this is of course one-sided. There was much more than foolishness in the author of *Anna Karenina* and *War and Peace*. I don't underestimate him or undervalue him —nor did Veresayev, who, though shocked to find him so much like "a rather rigid and dull Tolstoyan, contrary and inconsistent" (p. 308), continued to recognize the supreme greatness of his best novels. The genius of a great writer subsumes, modulates and transforms his foolishness as well as all the other elements of his character; but Tolstoy, unsatisfied by and perhaps dissatisfied with his imaginative works, was driven by his guilty demon to propound his foolishness unimaginatively, directly, raw, unmodulated, blatant; and its resonances, direct and reflected, continue to resound in the heads of socialist-realist hacks, age-of-Aquarius innocents, and missionary English teachers.

Something similar must be said of D. H. Lawrence. To call him simply a snob or an *arriviste* or a fascist sympathizer is not enough; it doesn't at all account for the high quality of his fiction or the fascination of his personality or the continuing influence of both on people who are neither unliterary nor illiberal. (For an example, see *The Autobiography of Bertrand Russell* [Boston: Atlantic–Little Brown, 1968], II, 10–16, 59–61.) But since he was one of the chief modern spokesmen for the notion that we should trust what we have in common with the rest of nature rather than what is distinctively human, and since his advocacy seems not to have been altogether disinterested or altogether unconnected with his *arrivisme,* we can legitimately limit this discussion to these non-literary aspects of his work.

105
The Noble
Savage;
or, Backing
Away from
Nature

[2] Adaline Glasheen writes, "Promoters of Noble Savagery are always men who hate women."

*Chapter 6
The Noble
Savage;
or, Backing
Away from
Nature*

The basic theme that underlies and unites all others in his fiction is the conflict of instinctive with conventional life, of "phallic consciousness" with "mental consciousness," and the corresponding conflict within himself. In *Sons and Lovers,* Paul's mother, having yielded to her husband's strong vital attraction, is repelled by the impropriety of his life, reasserts the values of cleanliness, godliness, etc., with at least equal strength, and in a long struggle gradually destroys him. Paul, true to the name his mother gave him, follows her rather than his father, overcomes his love for the farmer's daughter Miriam and the factory worker Clara, and, Mom being the only available lady of higher social origin, devotes himself to her as long as she lives; after her death he sets out to conquer ladies of higher rank in the larger world: as a gamekeeper, Connie Chatterley; as a dark Mexican, blue-eyed Irish Kate Leslie; as a dark Slavic private, a blue-eyed ladylike Prussian officer; as a medieval serf, Martha, the miller's daughter; as a horse (St. Lawr?), Lou Witt; as D. H. Lawrence, Frieda von Richtofen, Mabel Dodge Motors, Lady Ottoline Morrell, etc. This is the substance, more social than biological, of his famous Oedipus complex: if the Marxists hadn't rejected Freud, and with him all the light that shines from myths, they could see that the Oedipus myth can be read as Vico most probably would have read it—as a myth of class insurrection, of a feared and/or wished-for rising of the slaves or helots, the poor shepherd's son killing the king and taking his wife, but then (lest the bard be killed or the story not be accepted for publication) turning out to be a prince after all, like Tom Jones and how many others, including the beggar who won Odysseus' wife by force of arms. Such an interpretation would also explain the deeply conservative Lawrence's fascination with the beaked harpy and the vagina dentata, the guardian furies who put down insurrections and dark male risings.

The depth of his conservatism is indicated by a passage in Chapter IX of *The Plumed Serpent,* about the Mexican Indian peasant Ezequiel:

> Though he was just a hired labourer, yet, working on the land he never felt he was working for a master. It was the land he worked for. Somewhere inside himself he felt that the land was his, and he belonged in a measure to it. Perhaps a lingering feeling of tribal, communal land-ownership and service. . . .
>
> Only, when the Socialist Government had begun giving the peasants bits of land, dividing up the big haciendas, Ezequiel had been allotted a little piece outside the village. He would go and gather the stones together there, and prepare to build a little hut. And he would break the earth with a hoe, his only implement, as far as possible. But he had no blood connection with this square allotment of unnatural earth, and he could not get himself into relations with it. He was fitful and diffident about it. There was no incentive, no urge. [Vintage Books ed. (New York: Alfred A. Knopf, 1955), pp. 158–59.]

*107
The Noble
Savage;
or, Backing
Away from
Nature*

No incentive! The U.S. Chamber of Commerce can do as well as that! But Lawrence was not so absolute a fool as to believe what this passage with its loaded imagery and vocabulary, out of context, seems to say: that the earth became unnatural under socialist government, or that a self-respecting man, as he says Ezequiel was, could work for the master of a hacienda and not feel that he was working for a master, or actually feel that the land was somehow his, or that the hacienda was a tribal commune. What he means, the context states quite plainly: that it was not natural for Ezequiel, a member of a dark and therefore inferior race, to own land or be independent or work as anything other than a hired laborer or a servant:

Ah the dark races! Kate's own Irish were near enough, for her to have glimpsed some of the mystery. The dark races belong to a bygone cycle of humanity. They are left behind in a gulf out of which they have never been able to climb. They can only follow as servants.

Chapter 6
The Noble
Savage;
or, Backing
Away from
Nature

While the white man keeps the impetus of his own proud, onward march, the dark races will yield and serve, perforce. But let the white man once have a misgiving about his own leadership, and the dark races will at once attack him, to pull him down into the old gulfs. To engulf him again.

Which is what is happening. For the white man, let him bluster as he may, is hollow with misgiving about his own supremacy.

Full speed ahead, then, for the débâcle (p. 162).

(One thinks of the Taj Mahal.)

Kate's Gobineauvian pessimism is also Lawrence's own —*The Plumed Serpent* being a very preachy novel. He expressed that view repeatedly in his letters, veering back and forth between scorn of the dark races for lacking intellect and scorn of the white race for lacking sexual power—one penny cliché being as good as another. He trimmed his views on race to suit his correspondents, because racism was for him hardly more than a metaphor. To Lady Cynthia Asquith, after a visit to Ceylon, he writes, "The natives are *back* of us—in the living sense *lower* than we are. But they're going to swarm over us and suffocate us. . . . But you don't catch me going back on my whiteness and Englishness. English in the teeth of all the world, even in the teeth of England" (Diana Trilling, ed., *Selected Letters of D. H. Lawrence* [New York, Doubleday Anchor Books, 1961], p. 213). The key phrase here, as we shall see, is "even in the teeth of England." To Mabel Dodge, on the other hand, he writes repeatedly that her marriage with the Indian Tony Luhan is a good thing (pp. 198, 229), and when he himself has to return from Mexico to England he tells her it will be for a short time only: "Directly or indirectly I shall come back, this side, Mexico. I fight against the other side: Europe and the White and U.S." (p. 231).

What he fights against, however, is not the white race or the geographical areas it inhabits, but the movement toward social equality that had made it possible for his father to marry his mother: "My mother was a clever, ironical, delicately moulded woman of good, old burgher descent. She married below her" (p. 5). His works were metaphorical continuations and justifications of that struggle. His racism, his anti-Semitism (p. 257), even his naturism, were merely superficial metaphorical metamorphoses or chameleon disguises of his basic passion, which was social snobbery. Throughout his life, his highest word of praise for those he liked was "nice." The changes in his relationship with Mabel resulted (if you'll pardon a bit of sociologese) from the intersection of his upwardly mobile course with her downwardly mobile course.

How well he fooled himself with his disguises! Especially the disguise of naturism, which enabled him to play at once the irresponsible sensualist or coal miner's son and the defender of traditional Asquithian England. Pre-capitalist England. Feudal England. Although in one of his rare attempts at humor he said,

My mother was a superior soul,
A superior soul was she,
Out to play a superior role
In the god-damn bourgeoisie,

when he was being serious he called her descent "burgher," not bourgeois. At least since Lillo and Diderot, the word "bourgeois" has connoted, for better and for worse, economic and social ambition and getting on in the world, and a certain indifference to aristocratic

Chapter 6
The Noble
Savage;
or, Backing
Away from
Nature

assumptions of superiority: Baudelaire hated the bourgeois not because they were stuffy but because they were irreligious and unwilling to defer to the pre-bourgeois established order; Barbey d'Aurevilly hated them because they had perpetrated the Enlightenment; Mallarmé mocked them for presuming to read poetry and give their children piano lessons; but the word "burgher" connotes none of these things, only honest industry and settled contentment: God in His Heaven, the lord in his castle, the burgher in his shop, the peasant in the field, high-ho the derry-o. Lawrence was distressed by the destruction of this scheme and by the continuing social unsettlement, of which his parents' marriage was a symptom. His story "A Fragment of Stained Glass," with his word "No" at the end, indicates what he thought of devils who tried to break into Heaven. His story "The Horse Dealer's Daughter" expresses his own determination to avoid emotional involvement with strong, sensual, affectionate, passionate, mindless, natural-all-too-natural girls of his own class, even though in a letter to Edward Garnett he said women were naturally mindless and he preferred them that way (*Selected Letters,* p. 79); and Paul's relationship with Miriam in *Sons and Lovers* expresses Lawrence's determination to avoid emotional involvement with any girl, however sensitive and intelligent, of his own class. His contempt for democracy, his anti-humanitarianism, his anti-intellectualism, his vague utopian schemes for a society governed by natural aristocrats, his Baudelairean anti-Americanism, his Carlylean prayer for the silence of the governed, his Nietzschean dream of a superman (a role in which he sometimes saw himself: *Selected Letters,* pp. 232–33), his Jungian and anti-Freudian wish to let the id prevail unrestrained among natural rulers—this was the social basis of all his blood-thinking and naturism:

My great religion is a belief in the blood, the flesh, as being wiser than the intellect. We can go wrong in our minds. But what our blood feels and believes and says, is always true. The intellect is only a bit and a bridle. What do I care about knowledge. All I want is to answer to my blood, direct, without fribbling intervention of mind, or moral, or what-not. . . . That is why I like to live in Italy. The people are so unconscious. They only feel and want: they don't know. . . . The real way of living is to answer to one's wants. Not "I want to light up with my intelligence as many things as possible" but "For the living of my full flame—I want that liberty, I want that woman, I want that pound of peaches, I want to go to sleep, I want to go to the pub and have a good time, I want to look a beastly swell today, I want to kiss that girl, I want to insult that man." [Pp. 48–49.]

But he didn't at all approve of his father's efforts to live that way. He didn't want that fine free way of life for everybody. Not for hired laborers and servants. Only for their masters—the relationship of master and servant being as natural, he said, as that of man and woman; in fact, he thought the right relationship of man and woman was that of master and servant (*Selected Letters,* p. 169). As for servants and hired laborers, let them from time to time enjoy the communal ritual of seeing one of their number whipped, for no reason necessarily except that it gives the master pleasure. (See the essay on Dana's *Two Years Before the Mast* in Lawrence's *Studies in Classic American Literature* [New York: Doubleday Anchor Books, no date], pp. 128–32.) Lawrence's life and the whole body of his work illustrate not only the hypocritical uses to which naturism can be put but the radical incompatibility of the desire for a merely instinctive life with the desire for decent human relations.

Yeats also—with his belief that all true things are born

of instinct, coming into being as naturally as a long-legged fly walks on water—ignored his own practice of rewriting and rewriting and rewriting and rewriting and rewriting, and politicking and politicking and politicking. Nor did his Exupéry-like mystique of senseless danger-seeking ("An Irish Airman Foresees His Death") at all consist with his love of custom and ceremony, his support of the local storm-troopers, and his completely reactionary record as a Senator. Jean Giono likewise—whose blood-and-soil mysticism and lyric opposition to farm machinery ingratiated him with the occupying Nazis, who were hauling off all the machinery they could get their hands on—and Aldous Huxley, who promoted psychedelic incoherence and opposed public education, and most of the other naturizers of our time, have tended to support the sickest elements in our culture and to yearn back toward even sicker cultures.

*Chapter 6
The Noble
Savage;
or, Backing
Away from
Nature*

Prufrock's timid wish that he could stop measuring out his life with coffee spoons, and Molly Bloom's scorn for Leopold's "measuring and mincing" when he makes tea—"I always want to throw a handful of tea into the pot"—have a strong appeal, and it is a valid appeal. But not if you want a good cup of tea or coffee. And we do. So did Yeats. So did Lawrence. So did Giono. So do most writers, who by necessity of the life they have chosen spend most of their time indoors and sitting down, and whose friends tend to be not supermen with muscle-bound minds who go around knocking people down, but literate and sensitive men and women who share a writer's interests and values.

Nature is all right in its place, but its place is not all over the place. It is best when we view it in comfort from a comfortable distance:

>   . . . be mine the hut
> That from the mountain's side
> Views wilds and swelling floods,

but let's keep the roof repaired. And would you mind if I closed the window?

P.S.: As an antidote to this chapter I recommend George Orwell's essay on the coming of Spring, "Some Thoughts on the Common Toad."

113
The Noble
Savage;
or, Backing
Away from
Nature

7
The Evil Intellectual

          The Latin adjective *faustus* means "lucky." The most interesting character in *Waiting for Godot* is Lucky: Faustus in the modern world.

    The legend of Faustus, the evil intellectual, seems to have started with a historical character, the Manichean missionary Faustus, whom St. Augustine portrays in the *Confessions* (Book V, chs. 3, 6 and 7) as a charming faker who lectured eloquently but couldn't answer questions. The subsequent growth of the legend, through a wide variety of historical characters and literary treatments, shows Faustus sometimes as a charlatan (Paracelsus, John Dee, Marlowe's version), sometimes as a creative thinker (Erigena, Berengar, Roger Bacon, Goethe's version—and let us not forget that the German word *Faust* means fist), sometimes as both (Adrian Leverkühn, Oskar Matzerath); sometimes as victorious over Mephistopheles, sometimes as defeated by him; but always as a man of more than ordinary gifts and usually as a man of incomprehensible flimflam fluency. It is this fact, more than the coincidence of names, that makes Beckett's Lucky a Faust figure. For in the past, as the quality of his ruined diction shows, Lucky was an intellectual who expounded dilemmas with great self-confidence; perhaps he was a pedant, but if so he belonged to the rare subspecies of knowledgeable, clever and undogmatic pedants; in any case, nobody else in *Waiting for Godot* has attained the level of intellectual development at which pedantry becomes possible: not even Didi is the past Lucky's equal.

It would be easy enough to pull that battered old cliché "irony" out of the bag and call poor Lucky an anti-Faust. But in this case as in many others, we can have more fun playing a more complicated game.

In Goethe's version, Faust agrees to become a servant of Mephistopheles, instantly obedient to his slightest sign, if Mephistopheles can give him an experience that will fully satisfy him, thus ending his lifelong pursuit of new experiences. Toward the end of Part II Mephistopheles is about to succeed, but God, having predicted at the beginning of Part I that he would fail, kills Faust before the fully satisfying experience has time to occur, and sends a flight of angels to spirit his spirit away to Heaven. That is cheating. Beckett, however, a considerably harder man than Goethe, permits no cheating, even by his slickest student, who is of course God. So that what we have in *Waiting for Godot* is Faust in Hell as the servant of Mephistopheles. And he is perfectly satisfied: for this is the one experience that his arrangement with Mephistopheles had denied him above ground: absolute passive irresponsibility, "the freedom of indifference, the indifference of freedom, the will dust in the dust of its object, the act a handful of sand let fall" (*Murphy* [New York: Grove Press, 1957], p. 105). Lucky shows no sign of discontent except when Pozzo expresses a wish to get rid of him—then he weeps; he shows no sign of anger except when the well-disposed Gogo tries to wipe his tears away—then he kicks Gogo.

Even when he has the whip in his hand he doesn't rebel —he gives it obediently back to Pozzo. And he has entirely lost his intellect. He speaks from habit only, automatically, like a tape or a phonograph record on a badly damaged machine, reflexively, not reflectively. He is no longer capable of thought. His speech is that of a fine and complex mind fallen into a state of complete relaxation, moving only when it is ordered to. His syntax is much more sophisticated than that of anybody else in the play, but it no longer works, and he neither knows nor cares that it doesn't work. He is babbling, not thinking. He has lost the need to think. He has achieved the *summum bonum.* He is in Paradise.

We hate certain thinkers because they keep pulling us up out of the Paradise into which we keep trying to sink. They don't let us relax. We hate them because we see what they mean, or at least think we see what they mean. We don't hate all thinkers. We don't hate Einstein, for example, because we have no hope of understanding him. We hate Freud, because he showed us the id and the super-ego, which we would rather not see anyhow, and suggested that by understanding them we would have a better chance to resist their more bizarre suggestions and so develop more conscious control over our own behavior; we turn away from him to the anti-rationalist authoritarian Jung, who bade us yield to them because he knew that people who can't say no to a subliminal suggestion are easier to manipulate than those who can.

This is of course an oversimplification, and a very bad oversimplification, because if it were the whole truth there would be no hope for us. We would be trolls. But we are not trolls. At least, not all the time. Our nature is complex and many-sided. The need to think is an important element in our nature, and we do in fact honor, if only with our outraged attention, those who most conspicuously illustrate and represent it. For we

are neither apes nor angels; nor do we serve
Mephistopheles in abject ataraxia.

The Evil Intellectual fascinates us, therefore, for
essentially the same reason that the Wicked City
fascinates us. He/she shows us possibilities, both for
good and for evil, both within ourselves and beside
ourselves. The intellectual, like the city, intoxicates us,
drives us mad, with possibilities.

The prototype was of course not Faustus but
Mephistopheles' commander, Satan. We have it on the
very best authority (Genesis 3) that it was he who
opened the eyes of the human race. He was the genuine
article; but the heathen had some pretty good imitations.
Hephaestus, who like Satan was thrown out of Heaven
(twice, in fact), became a fire-god and the first ingenious
artificer, inventor of ceramics, metallurgy, leg braces and
the automobile. He was the first crippled creator. He
prostituted his gifts, however: having been received back
into Heaven, he made the chains that bound
Prometheus, another fire-god, whom Zeus reproached
with being "deep-minded" and "cunning." (See Robert
Graves, *The Greek Myths*, sec. 23; for a more detailed
account, see Marie Delcourt's *Héphaistos, ou La Légende du
Magicien* [Paris: Société d'Edition "Les Belles Lettres"],
1957.)

What Zeus chiefly resented in Prometheus was not his
giving fire to us human beings but his teaching us
"architecture, astronomy, mathematics, navigation,
medicine, metallurgy, and other useful arts" (Graves,
sec. 39 *e*). Many creation myths show the gods resenting
human intelligence, lest we rival their power or at least
not be completely subject to it: lest we develop the
ability to govern our own affairs more or less well. Satan
is represented as tempting us with the statement, "ye
shall be as gods, knowing good and evil" (Genesis 3:5);
and when we undertook to build a tower to Heaven God
deliberately confused our speech so that we couldn't
work together (Genesis 11:1–9).

The tower was to have been surrounded by a city. That would have been the second human city. The first was Enoch, founded by Cain, the first murderer, when he was cast out from the human race; and his descendants were the first artists, artisans and craftsmen (Genesis 4:17–22). Rome also was built by a fratricide, Romulus having killed Remus shortly after the work began. And in early Christian allegory, Athens, the City of Man, was set over against Jerusalem, the City of God.

Tertullian, the first of the Latin Fathers, in a famous diatribe against philosophy, said, "What has Jerusalem to do with Athens? Or the Church with the Academy? Or Christians with heretics? . . . Curiosity is not for us, since we have Christ Jesus; nor investigation, since we have the Gospel" (*Liber de Praescriptionibus Adversus Haereticos,* VII, in Migne, *Patrologia Latina,* II, 20 B, 21 A; cf. II Corinthians 6:14–16). The more sophisticated St. Augustine said that since the liberal arts are neutral, and can be turned to either good or bad uses, Christians should cultivate them and use them for the confuting of heretics (*De Doctrina Christiana,* IV, 2, in Migne, XXXIV, 89 [D]–90[A]; *De Musica,* VI, xvii, 59, in Migne, XXXII, 1194[A]). These two attitudes have continued to prevail, respectively, among the more naive and the more sophisticated conservatives, not only in religion but also in government and even in education. Neither naive nor sophisticated conservatives care for independent thinkers who are not committed in advance to avoid finding out anything unsettling. A twentieth-century fantast—Pinget? Borges? I forget—tells about a country that had an ignorant academy of sciences, an inaccurate observatory, and a false calendar; its king was quite aware of those deficiencies, but refused to do anything to correct them, because once you start changing things, there's no stopping—and besides, he didn't want to undermine the people's confidence in himself.

That is the basic conservative attitude. But it is not limited to kings. We, the people, are also afflicted with it. We are often timid. We often distrust ourselves. Often, not by conscious choice but by default of will or psychic energy, we choose to bear those ills we have. By a chosen, voluntary, self-inflicted incapacity, we *cannot* desire to change anything. We have what Hugh of St. Victor (1096–1141) called "initial fear"—a disabling fear he advised us to cultivate because it operates in our inmost depths and makes us unable to have an unorthodox thought (Hugh of St. Victor, *On the Sacraments of the Christian Faith*, trans. Roy J. Deferrari [Cambridge, Mass.: The Medieval Academy of America, 1951], pp. 377–78). He was speaking of religious orthodoxy; but initial fear keeps us orthodox in secular matters also. We don't have to cultivate it; if we are comfortably well off—and even more if we are just on the precarious edge of middle-class comfort and respectability, so that any prospect of unsettlement seems to threaten us—our position in society tends to make unorthodoxy literally unthinkable and unfeelable. Hence the notorious puzzling fact that many poor exploited clerks are at least as conservative as the employers who exploit them; hence the notorious puzzling fact that many industrial workers, having achieved modestly decent incomes, vote for conservative candidates with records of consistent opposition to the interests of workers and consumers; and hence the notorious puzzling fact that intellectuals who try to persuade them to look at the candidates' voting records are often regarded as devils tempting them to sin: to fall.

There are several reasons for their suspicion of the man or woman who hands them a table showing how members of Congress voted on specific bills.

1. From initial fear rather than from any lack of mental ability, they are disinclined to do much close reading of political or social facts: not only may the material at hand undermine their faith in safe beliefs, but any appearance of intellectuality is politically suspect. When the House Judiciary Committee was debating

articles of impeachment against Richard Nixon, liberal as well as conservative members of the committee pretended to have difficulty with the word "specificity." One, who after several efforts finally pronounced it right, laughed and said, "I wish I hadn't."

2. A belief based on emotion affords a certain physiological pleasure through the release of adrenalin, be the emotion anger or conviviality, love or hate, blood lust or fear; the colorless tabulation of facts in a voting record, appealing to emotion only indirectly if at all, threatens to rob of a pleasure the followers of a demagogue. Since they love him, the fact that he consistently votes against their interests doesn't interest them.

3. The uninvited emissary of a different culture, approaching us with missionary intent, threatens our culture, our souls, our selves.

4. There is a long tradition, of which we are all more or less dimly aware, that verbal precision—i.e., clarity of thought—is irreligious. In the middle ages grammar was taught by ecclesiastics or not at all; nevertheless, there were repeated ecclesiastical complaints against such teaching and such study. I quote three out of many. Pope Gregory I (c. 540–604) wrote in some perturbation to Desiderius, Bishop of Gaul:

> . . . It afterwards came to our ears—we cannot mention it without shame—that certain of your fraternity are in the habit of teaching grammar. Which thing we took so much amiss, and were so deeply disturbed by it, that we changed our previous words into groaning and sadness. . . . If hereafter what has been reported to us should prove false, and if it should be clear that you do not apply your mind to trifles and to secular letters, we shall give thanks to our God. [Migne, *Patrologia Latina,* LXXVII, 1171 C, 1172 A.]

Peter Damian (1007–72) said that monks who studied grammar were adulterers, and those who taught them pimps:

> There are two kinds of monks of whom I admittedly speak with anger. The first are those who run with the rabble of grammarians, who, having abandoned spiritual studies, lust to learn the folly of worldly arts: despising the rule of Benedict [founder of Western monasticism] and delighting in the rules of Donatus [a fourth-century Roman grammarian]. Moreover, disdaining skill in the discipline of the church but greedily gaping for secular studies, what do they do but forsake their chaste spouse in the bridechamber of the faith and openly descend to showy prostitutes? The second, let it be confessed, are those who serve as pimps and freely grant divorces to those who delight in whoredom, that they may in shameful violation of their marriage associate with slave girls. [A standard metaphor in medieval schools was that the liberal arts were *ancillae*—servants—of Theology, Queen of the Sciences.] [Migne, CXLV, 306 C.]

And Richard of St. Victor (d. 1173)—Richard, that is, not Hugh—complained that many university students "are more ashamed to commit a barbarism against a rule of Priscian [a sixth-century grammarian of Constantinople] than to tell a lie against the rule of Christ" (Migne, CXCVI, 34 C; cf. St. Augustine, *Confessions,* I, 30: "I feared more to commit a barbarism, than having committed one, to envy those who had not" —E. B. Pusey, trans.).

These objectors were neither stupid nor consciously disingenuous. Their objections were based on three facts:

1. Time devoted to secular subjects, beyond the necessary minimum for their status as service subjects,

tended to be subtracted from the time devoted to the higher study, theology. Chaucer's Clerk of Oxenford was one of many students who "un-to logik hadde long y-go," postponing or abandoning the study of theology. This tendency worried the educational and ecclesiastical authorities no end.

2. Secular knowledge is and always will be incomplete. Therefore, since the means tend to become the end, awareness of its incompleteness tends to stimulate intellectual activity for its own sake. St. Augustine called secular knowledge for its own sake vain and foolish, the desire for it a concupiscence of the soul, and the pursuit of it a disease (*Confessions,* X, 54–55). Secular study encourages tentativeness of conclusion and modesty of assertion, but the aim of religious study is unshakable conviction; the respective psychological dispositions are inherently incompatible. Endless pursuit of additional evidence for the faith, yes; endless pursuit of knowledge for its own sake, without a predetermined orthodox conclusion, no.

3. As Genesis indicates, knowledge is also incompatible with moral innocence. Aristotle said much the same thing: in art it is better to err intentionally than unintentionally, but in morality it is less bad to err unintentionally (*Nicomachean Ethics,* 1140 b). Neither Genesis nor Aristotle, however, is to blame for the familiar demagogic assertion of moral rectitude and intellectual harmlessness, "Yes, I've made mistakes, but they was mistakes of the head, not of the heart." Much less is either to blame for the demagogic corollary that precision of thought is wicked. Timidity is a weakness we must always struggle against. Especially organized and aggressive timidity.

In addition to these three objections to worldly knowledge, a few sensitive spirits have always adduced a fourth, which is of a different psychological kind. The taming of the wild and innocent Enkidu, in the myth of Gilgamesh, associates the beginning of civilization with sin. The ecstatic Richard Rolle (1290–1349) said, "Lovers of the world can understand the words or verses of our song, but not the song of our verses"; he mocked his intellectual detractors as "dullards, not imbued with divine wisdom but puffed up with acquired knowledge" (C. Horstman ed., *Yorkshire Writers: Richard Rolle of Hampole and his Followers* [2 vols., London: Swan Sonnenschein & Co., 1896], II, xxx). They are wrong, he said, because (having no intuitive gifts) they reject intuition, the only source of divine wisdom; "I, Richard, the so-called solitary hermit, know better, because I have experienced it; and what I know, I maintain."

We increasingly run into this kind of thing now: the claims of intuitive wisdom, incommunicable but infallible. When they are couched in semi-literate commonplaces they are easy enough to refute; they are in fact usually couched in semi-literate commonplaces, and have no other fruits to show; everybody who knows anything knows that the quality of a poem cannot be inferred from the intensity of emotional pleasure the poet experienced while writing it—as Joyce would say, we are concerned with the written word; but now and then we come upon written words whose high quality cannot be accounted for in terms of anything learnable. As my son Jonathan once pointed out to me, "Edna St. Vincent Millay observed the textbook rules of versification and Emily Dickinson didn't, but Emily was a superb technician and Edna was none." Who taught Samuel Beckett to write? In what rulebook did he find rules for the singing phrases I have quoted on page 115? Books of classical rhetoric do indeed give rules, patterns, paradigms, and it's too bad we no longer read them; Beckett himself is a master of classical rhetoric, as the formal elegance of Lucky's babbling shows; but no rules account for him, and there are no conceivable rules for being Beckett. Or Emily Dickinson. Richard Rolle was right: the singing of a great writer's language is not something that can be consciously learned or taught. He was neither the first nor the last to say it. Homer said it, when he invited the Muse, without whom there is no singing. Plato said it, in *Ion* and again in *Phaedrus;* Shakespeare's Theseus said it, in *A Midsummer Night's Dream;* etc., etc. Addison, for example, said it, in *The Spectator,* no. 592: insensitive critics

are often led into those numerous absurdities in which they daily instruct the people by not considering that, first, there is sometimes a greater judgment shown in deviating from the rules of art than in adhering to them; and, secondly, that there is more beauty in the works of a great genius who is ignorant of all the rules of art than in the works of a little genius who not only knows, but scrupulously observes them.

First, we may often take notice of men who are perfectly acquainted with all the rules of good writing, and notwithstanding choose to depart from them on extraordinary occasions. I could give instances of all the tragic writers of antiquity who have shown their judgment in this particular, and purposely receded from an established rule of the drama when it has made way for a much higher beauty than the observation of such a rule would have been. . . .

In the next place, our critics do not seem sensible that there is more beauty in the works of a great genius who is ignorant of the rules of art than in those of a little genius who knows and observes them. . . . Our inimitable Shakespeare is a stumbling-block to the whole tribe of these rigid critics. Who would not rather read one of his plays, where there is not a single rule of the stage observed, than any production of a modern critic where there is not one of them violated!

Addison, however, fell into the equally common opposite error. There has never been a great genius who was ignorant of the rules of his/her art. Every great genius has either learned the rules or independently rediscovered or re-invented them; and his/her departures from them have been not fallings short but goings beyond: the achievement of unique technical brilliancies. The opening scene of *Hamlet,* for example, is technically brilliant beyond any conceivable rulebook prescription. Shakespeare had long since mastered all the prescriptions; the Restoration and Augustan notion that he hadn't was a fashionable prejudice indicating superficial or no observation. Independent close observation would have shown Addison and other fashionable critics that in *A Comedy of Errors* Shakespeare had strictly observed "the rules," that in *Hamlet* he disregarded them from time to time deliberately, not ignorantly, and that in the speeches of Polonius, the Player King, and Rosencrantz and Guildenstern, he parodied and mocked the traditions he had mastered. That is quite a different thing from automatic writing. The Muse is, as André Spire observed, hidden in subconscious depths; but—as his historical investigations showed—the intuitions of genius don't come to the untrained. (See André Spire, *Plaisir Poétique et Plaisir Musculaire* [New York: S.F. Vanni, 1949]; I translated Chapter II, a key chapter, as an appendix to my textbook of writing, *Matters of Style* [Indianapolis: Bobbs-Merrill, 1968]).

Geniuses—all of them, without exception—constantly practice their art, endlessly refine their techniques. Their innovations are the technical experiments of experts pushing against the outer limits of their art, not the fumbling of beginners or complacent ignoramuses who haven't mastered the rudiments. I emphasize this obvious point because there is now, as there is from time to time, a return of another form of anti-intellectualism, that of naive souls who think their "free-form" scribbles or squiggles express something other than lack of technique. As if every belch were a song, every tape-recorded squeaking of a door a sonata, every stumble an entrechat, every random jumble of words a poem, every blowing of cigarette smoke a masterpiece of sculpture, every lean-to a revolutionary breakthrough in experimental architecture, every crying jag a contribution to metaphysics. These innocents consider anything more artful insincere. The best that can be said of them is that their mistakes are mistakes of the head. Their statements show nothing but ignorance and incoherence; they seem hardly capable of serious argument, and there is a temptation not to take them seriously: not to reply to their formless babbling. There is also a temptation, for other reasons, not to reply to their few articulate supporters, opportunists who know better. But since we run into them everywhere, and since their notions promise such a dim future, for art, for thought, for accountable government, and for the condition of us common people, we must not leave them unanswered.

8

The Alienated Artist

On May 14, 1877, Rimbaud wrote to the American Consul in Bremen, in English, as follows:

Bremen the 14 mai 77 [*sic*]
The untersigned [*sic*] Arthur Rimbaud—Born in Charleville (France)—Aged 23—5 ft. 6 height—Good healthy [*sic*] —Late a teacher of sciences and languages—Recently deserted from the 47ᵉ Regiment of the French Army,—Actually [i.e., *actuellement:* at present] in Bremen without any means, the French Consul refusing any relief.

Would like to know on which terms he could conclude an immediate engagement in the American navy.

Speaks and writes English, French, German, Italian and Spanish.

Has been four months as a sailor in a Scotch bark, from Java to Queenstown, from August to December 76, [*sic*]

Would be very honoured and grateful to receive an answer.

John Arthur Rimbaud

It wasn't the French army he had deserted from, incidentally, but the Dutch army, in which he had enlisted as a mercenary in order to get to Java. But no matter. From an ordinary person such a letter would be merely stupid; from a man of Rimbaud's genius it is insane. He is a prize example of mad and criminal genius. It is easy enough to think of other geniuses who were mad or criminal or both: Rimbaud's boyfriend Verlaine; Villon; Dostoievsky; Nietzsche; Strindberg; Gérard de Nerval; Céline; Léon Bloy—to mention only writers. It is also easy to think of geniuses who, though not actually mad or criminal, were unmistakably neurotic: Pope, Swift, Sterne, Poe, Baudelaire, Heine, Proust, Kafka, Veblen. But it is even easier to think of geniuses who led quite sane and respectable bourgeois lives and were fully appreciated in their own times—because there have been many more of them.

To believe that in the post-feudal post-monarchical more or less democratic modern world most geniuses are out of place, unsocial, anti-social, sick, insane, criminal, etc., is to believe with Baudelaire that democratic society has no use for people of superior ability and would rather not have them around: "Nations have no great men but despite themselves—like families. They do everything they can to avoid having any. Thus, the great man, in order to exist, needs an aggressive strength greater than the strength of resistance developed by millions of individuals" (*Fusées,* VII). To believe that is to believe that democracy is incompatible with excellence. There are people who do believe that democracy is incompatible with excellence. Some frankly say they believe in aristocratic government—which is to say, practically speaking, in hereditary classes; others call themselves populists—which is to say, practically speaking, that they think trash is good enough for us common people and that anybody who thinks it isn't is a snob.

They are wrong. Anybody who has any acquaintance with intellectual history or cultural history knows that they are wrong. As a matter of statistical fact, most of the artists we now recognize as good were recognized as good by their contemporaries and got along quite well; nor was their success always limited to their art, nor did their art necessarily express or indicate an unusual degree of neurosis. As the old Quaker saying goes, we are all more or less nuts, including me and thee, but it doesn't incapacitate us.

Chaucer and Goethe, for example, were hard-working high-ranking public officials with major responsibilities, which they executed well; François Rabelais, M.D., was director of a hospital; Shakespeare left Stratford poor at 21 and returned rich at 33, the most popular and most highly respected playwright of his time; Dickens, Balzac, Hugo, Zola, Flaubert, Mark Twain, Joseph Conrad, Tolstoy, Nabokov and Thomas Mann all wrote great novels that were best-sellers because large numbers of us common people enjoy great novels; the mad Dostoievsky's great novels also were best-sellers; Ibsen got rich writing great plays; so did Lillian Hellman—on Broadway and in Hollywood, no less; Chekhov and de Maupassant did very well financially writing great short stories; in the French educational system, where professional promotion is through rigorous subject-matter exams designed to eliminate most candidates, Sartre and Simone de Beauvoir both became professors of philosophy before they wrote best-selling books dealing seriously with the most serious issues of our time; Nathalie Sarraute was a successful lawyer, as well as a mother, before she began writing serious novels that became best-sellers; Alain Robbe-Grillet was a successful agronomist, an expert on tropical fruits, and a propagandist who succeeded in popularizing pineapples in France; Michel Butor was a well-known professor of English; William Carlos Williams, one of our better American poets, was a busy and prosperous M.D.; Wallace Stevens, probably the best poet this country has produced since Whitman (who incidentally was a successful newspaper editor), started out as a Wall Street corporation lawyer, became vice-president in charge of the legal department of the Hartford Accident and Indemnity Company, and in supplying biographical information for *Who's Who in America* wrote after his name not "poet" but "insurance."

Many of these, moreover, were quite consciously bourgeois. Thomas Mann called himself, not altogether ironically, "a bourgeois story-teller"; and Dickens sometimes had to remind contributors to *Household Words,* a magazine he owned and edited, that certain scenes or incidents wouldn't do, because it was a family magazine.

One last illustration. The Austrian poet Georg Trakl (1887–1914), a drunkard and an opium addict, who committed incest with his sister, and at age 27 committed suicide by drinking ether, wrote some uniquely beautiful poems; but the Austrian poet Hugo von Hoffmannsthal (1874–1929), who lived a comfortable bourgeois life, wrote more and better poems —as well as excellent and successful plays, libretti and essays.

Then why does the myth persist that artists are mad or criminal or at least bohemian and irresponsible? Why do we generalize the relatively few who are, rather than the relatively many who are not?

There is no necessary conflict between art and the rest of life, any more than there is between business and the rest of life, or medicine and the rest of life, or engineering and the rest of life. To be sure, a person who devotes most of his or her time to one interest tends to become one-sided or lopsided, but a pianist who spends eight or more hours a day playing the piano, or a novelist who spends eight or more hours a day writing, is no nuttier than a PR man who spends eight or more hours a day promoting fascism or whatever else he is paid to promote, or a stock broker who spends eight or more hours a day buying and selling stocks. We are all more or less lopsided in our interests, our activities, our conversation, but it doesn't bother us, because we recognize that lopsidedness is the normal human condition. What bothers us in genius is not the specialization, which is no narrower than our own, but the inexplicable uniqueness of the results. We feel intuitively—and we are right—that geniuses differ from us not only in degree but also in kind. A genius is not merely a person with a great deal more knowledge or ability than we have, whom we might hope to match by long study, practice and development. He or she has something inexplicable and unaccountable, which no amount of study, practice and development will ever enable us even to approximate. There are many intellectuals, but few Columbuses of thought; many highly talented people of all kinds, but few geniuses. What should I do in order to become Sigmund Freud? Tell me, teacher. What should I do in order to compose like Mozart? Tell me, tell me! Give me the rules! Nobody can tell us. There are no rules. Many people can play the piano without hitting wrong notes, but only André Watts can play like André Watts and only Artur Rubinstein can play like Artur Rubinstein. There is no formula, no transmissible technique, for the singularity of genius. Nor are geniuses interchangeable. Wordsworth could count syllables as well as Pope; as far as textbook rules go, the heroic couplets of his early poems—e.g., "An Evening Walk" and "Descriptive Sketches"—are as correct as Pope's; but Wordsworth couldn't have written anything to match "The Rape of the Lock" if he had tried all day every day as long as he lived; and neither could Pope have written anything to match "I wandered lonely as a cloud" or "She lived among the untrodden ways." It took Wordsworth some time to find his own voice; and even after he found it, as we know, it came and went; but when he had it, he had a miraculous personal gift that nobody else has ever had, before or since. That is what genius is: a developed and cultivated miraculous personal gift. Assiduity is of course necessary; but assiduity alone won't produce the miracle.

The hero of Günter Grass's play *The Wicked Cooks* is a count, a gentleman cook, who makes a wonderful gray soup that tastes so good it gives those who eat it an ineffable joy. Some wicked cooks try, by means of threats, cajolery and bribery, to get the recipe out of him; but there is no recipe. As he tells them, to their bewilderment and cynical disbelief, he has never made the soup the same way twice, it's an expression of his life, of himself, continuously changing like Heraclitus' stream into which nobody can step twice. There are, to be sure, recipes, formulas, static standard procedures, which ordinary cooks can follow and make pretty good soup or even excellent soup; but there is no recipe for being Escoffier or Brillat-Savarin or Günter Grass's count.

But geniuses in fields other than the arts—comic-book and sci-fi mad scientists notwithstanding—are not popularly believed to be as a rule mad or criminal, much less bohemian; whereas artists are, even those who are not geniuses. Why? There are seven identifiable reasons, of which six are fairly plausible; but the seventh, which is itself mad and in its inherent nature criminal, as well as ludicrous, is the most important one for us to be aware of.

1. Plato's Socrates says (*Phaedrus* 244) that the words *mania*, madness, and *mantia*, prophecy, are merely different forms of the same word; that poets, like prophets, are mouthpieces for divinity; that their utterances are often hard to understand in merely rational human terms, and that they themselves can't

give any rational account of how they achieve such
utterance or even of what it means. This old tradition
gives poetry a certain mystic glamor; and since the Muse
is in fact hidden in subconscious depths, poets and other
artists are often tempted to play the role assigned to
them by popular superstition. Bad poets are especially
prone to this role—Robert Desnos, before going to bed
at night or taking a nap by day, hung a sign on his door,
"The poet is working"; and Robert de Montesquiou told
his servants, "If you hear me moaning, it means I am
writing poetry and am not to be disturbed."[1] Even good
ones sometimes do a little ridiculous play-acting—think
of Walt Whitman with that butterfly tied to his finger,
and Rimbaud deliberately setting out, as he said, to
shock the bourgeois. Picasso, who left an estate of more
than $750,000,000, didn't care whether people approved
of the way he dressed or not. He looked and acted and
was bohemian; and his paintings and sculptures
encouraged people who knew nothing about painting or
sculpture to think he was crazy. Too bad for them.

2. Not all artists are Picassos, Goethes, Chaucers,
Shakespeares, etc. Many of them, including some good
ones and even a few real geniuses, for various reasons,
live and die poor; and poverty, though by no means
identical with bohemianism, does have some obvious
affinities with it. An artist who can't sell his work, and
who has no other source of income, is poor in the same
way that an unemployed factory worker is poor: i.e., he
hasn't got any money. But somehow we think or rather
feel that the poverty of artists is charming and not really
painful. Its cliché symbol is a candle stuck in a wine
bottle. Its cliché dramatic representation is the opening
scene of Puccini's *La Bohème* (1896). But Henri Mürger,
who wrote *Scènes de la Vie de Bohème* (1848), the novel on
which the opera is based, knew better. Read his preface.

---

[1] Of dandies there are very few to match Robert de Montesquiou, and
specimens are even fewer at once so dandy and so pewer.

3. Plato's Socrates (*Republic* 377–403) was right: art *is* immoral, both because it encourages unsocial and anti-social attitudes and because it misrepresents reality. When we read *Crime and Punishment* we find ourselves sympathizing with an axe murderer and hoping he won't be caught. The reason, as my friend Maurice English has observed, is that the axe murderer is endowed with the sensibility of a Dostoievsky, which makes him an extremely unlikely axe murderer. When we read *Lolita* we find ourselves sympathizing with a criminal creep who is guilty of kidnapping, statutory rape, murder, and driving on the wrong side of the road; we sympathize with him because he writes like a humane and highly civilized scholar, with humor, irony, compassion, etc.—a rather unlikely creep.

4. Artists also portray sympathetically impulses and activities that though not criminal are . . . well, read this contribution to *The Anglo-Saxon Chronicle;* whether true or false, it was certainly written by a writer with the soul of a poet:

> A. 891: This year . . . three Scots came to king Alfred in a boat without any oars from Ireland, whence they had stolen away, because they desired for the love of God to be in a state of pilgrimage, they recked not where. The boat in which they came was made of two hides and a half; and they took with them provisions for seven days; and then about the seventh day they came ashore in Cornwall, and soon after went to king Alfred. [J. A. Giles trans. (London: George Bell & Sons, 1894), p. 325.]

The time of year is not stated, but I hope it was Spring. Undoubtedly there was wanderlust; undoubtedly there was also religious feeling, and reckless joy. Certainly there was a fine disregard of the way of the world, a folly to warm the heart of Erasmus. Even though the trip did end tamely at the royal court—an anticlimax and a disappointment for us readers—it was not quite analogous to those of the bold sailors who in our own time make long voyages in small boats; it seems to have been more an impulsive act of religious men than a deliberate undertaking, after long training and careful calculation, of sportsmen. Artists sympathize with such impulses.

5. Geniuses in other fields are much less likely to sympathize with them. It is not likely that a financial genius, a Rockefeller, an Onassis, a Vanderbilt—a person whose intuitive nature is such that everything he touches turns to money—would have any use for those three Scots. A scientific genius—an Oppenheimer, a Bertrand Russell—would certainly understand and sympathize with them; nevertheless, Oppenheimer and Russell were both members of the establishment, as most scientific geniuses nowadays in fact are; those Scots were evidently not, and the poets who celebrate such adventures are celebrating something the establishment can't take seriously. What does that make the poets?

(The fact that the establishment sometimes courts the favor of stupid vulgarians such as Joe McCarthy and Richard Nixon by vilifying its own most brilliant and morally sensitive members is a related matter.)

6. As my wife points out, geniuses in other fields work among and with and for and on other people, but artists work alone. Writers and composers necessarily work alone; many painters and sculptors enjoy company when they are working, and carry on lively conversations; even so, we have observed, they are giving only superficial and intermittent attention to the conversation. The focus of their interest is on the work; they can converse only because the work is not verbal; as social beings, they converse; as painters and sculptors, each is alone with the work.

7. The seventh reason, the insane one, makes no sense at all; but we should be aware of it, and beware of it, because it is a very widespread superstition—the belief

that a taste for the arts is unmanly and a sign of biological degeneracy.

Arthur Gobineau, in his *Essai sur l'inégalité des races humaines* (1853–55), stated dogmatically that the organizing intelligence that creates civilization is a monopoly of the white races, which alone are endowed with reason; that they are proportionately lacking in aesthetic sensitivity, and that therefore, unless their "blood" is mixed with that of other—i.e., of inferior— races, they have no capacity to create or even to enjoy works of art. Aesthetic sensitivity, he said, is characteristic of the blacks, as rational intelligence is of the whites; but the blacks, being totally devoid of rational intelligence, cannot control or organize their aesthetic responses. Art is possible, therefore, only when the aesthetic sensitivity of the blacks is combined in a mixed race with the organizing intelligence of the whites. What is stupid about this dogmatically stated view is that it is altogether conjectural and takes no account of obvious everyday facts—the fact, e.g., that in all races there are wide ranges of individual difference; and the fact that the whole history of the arts contradicts it.

But mere facts don't interest a nut who has thunk up a nutty idea. History, according to Gobineau, is the story of the successive conquests of the darker races, whom he calls "feminine," by lighter ones, whom he calls "masculine." After each such conquest the races mingle, the arts flourish, and the "masculine" civilization of the whites is softened by the "feminine" sensitivity of the blacks, until in time it becomes too soft to resist the onslaught of a lighter—that is, a superior—race. The white or civilizing races being physically, mentally and morally superior to all others—and even better looking— civilizations decline for one reason only: biological degeneracy. A taste for the arts is therefore a bad sign. With apocalyptic self-pity, Gobineau concludes that all the white races are now "tainted," and that all civilization will ultimately go down in racial darkness.

In 1967 I discovered that this notion underlay Thomas Mann's theory of the artist nature, and discussed its influence on his work at some length in "Gobineau and Thomas Mann" (*Helen Adolf Festschrift*, ed. Sheema Z. Buehne, James L. Hodge and Lucille B. Pinto [New York: Frederick Ungar, 1968], pp. 252–67). More recently, reading Thomas F. Gossett's *Race: The History of an Idea in America* (Dallas: Southern Methodist University Press, 1963; New York: Schocken Books, 1965, pp. 198–227), I have learned that such American writers as Owen Wister and Frank Norris as well as Jack London were influenced by Gobineau in the same way, whether or not they had read him: his notions hung like a miasma in the American air. For such popular writers to celebrate insensitivity—suggesting, as Gossett says they did, that the arts are for women only, and that self-respecting Nordic males can't even carry a tune— indicates that there was a large market for such pseudo-populism: a market of generally well-meaning people unaware of the aristocratic origins of hostility to the aesthetic impulse.

The curious notion that there are masculine and feminine races was too obviously crazy to catch on—but even it pops up here and there. Gobineau presented it again in *La fleur d'or* (1877); the romantic medievalist Henry Adams, in *Mont-Saint-Michel and Chartres* (1905), said (though I oversimplify) that the eleventh-century abbey of Mont-Saint-Michel was masculine in its architecture and dedicated to Saint Michael because it was built by a masculine race, the civilizing Normans, and that the thirteenth-century cathedral of Chartres was feminine in its architecture and dedicated to the Virgin Mary because it was built by a feminine race, the French, after the civilizing Normans had penetrated them; the polite Nazi officer in Vercors' anti-Nazi novella *Le silence de la mer* (1941) proposed a marriage between "feminine" France and "masculine" Germany—he politely suggested that France should accept marriage in order to make rape unnecessary; and—since conquest always involves rape—Livy's account of the rape of the Sabines, and the various Greek myths of the war with the Amazons, which involved the planting of colonies, can be read euhemeristically as reflections of conquest; but modern apologists for imperialism have not often deluded themselves with a metaphor that is so hard to take literally.

The metaphor of the artist as a person of mixed race, doubtful sex and doubtful civic virtue, however, which Gobineau and writers influenced by him did so much to propagate, is widespread indeed; and we should not take lightly the resulting prejudice against artists. It is analogous to the prejudices against women, intellectuals, Jews, and the darker races; equally insidious; equally dangerous to democratic society. All these and all other such prejudices are interlocked, each supporting and supported by all the others. The moral for us who believe in personal freedom would seem to be fairly obvious; nevertheless, we often find it safer to turn against each other, indulging the prejudices with which the establishment has endowed us, than to unite against the established prejudices of the prejudiced establishment.

9

The Brotherhood of Man

"Confirm thy good in brotherhood,"
we sing on ceremonial occasions.

In what?

We often hear the term "the brotherhood of man"
solemnly uttered, but we never hear it seriously
discussed or clearly defined. It doesn't seem to lend
itself. In what kinds of gatherings could it be discussed,
and how serious could such discussion be? I feel some
embarrassment in proposing "the brotherhood of man"
as a subject for clear definition to the readers of this
book.

The reason it seems to lack intellectual substance is
that it tempts the innocent into thoughtless acceptance
and the thoughtful into wistful denial. Those who
solemnly say "All men are brothers" say it as if it were a
statement of fact, whereas anybody who has any
knowledge of language knows that it is a metaphor.

But is the metaphor invalid? Or does it have some
basis in fact, so that we can give it a demonstrable

meaning that people who think with some precision can accept? If so, what? The statement doesn't easily lend itself to any literal reading. There is an ambiguity in the word "men," a word that means not only "adult human males" but also "human beings, without regard to age or sex." The word "brothers" sometimes has a similar ambiguity: such churches as the Church of the Brethren and the United Brethren have women members, so that the word "Brethren" implies "and Sistren" in the same way that "he" often implies "or she."

Thus the statement "All men are brothers," if we were to take it literally, would mean "All human beings are siblings," which takes us one step—one step too far—into the unreal world of sociologese, a jargon that falsifies everything human by referring to human beings as if they were algebraic symbols. (What sex is a sibling, for example? Have you ever seen one?) If the statement "All men are brothers" has any literal meaning at all, it means "All human beings are brothers and sisters." I don't know anybody who would take that statement seriously as a statement of fact. For one thing, it would make marriage impossible under our present laws.

It is a metaphor and nothing but a metaphor. There is no conceivable way to read it literally and have it make sense. Even if we take it to mean literally that we are all descendants of Adam and Eve, or of whatever pair was named in any other early story, it doesn't make sense, because as descendants of such far-away ancestors we are not brothers and sisters but cousins, and by now rather distant cousins. As a matter of fact, as I indicated in Chapter 2, many of us don't recognize each other even as human beings, much less as cousins. So that the statement "All men are brothers" doesn't make sense except as a metaphor. And what is the meaning of the statement "It makes sense as a metaphor"? What does that statement mean in terms of action and behavior?

It means that many of us have a rather large emotional investment in that metaphor: we are committed to it, in the same way that many people are committed to belief in God, or in a dialectical process of history, or in some other moving force or consistent pattern: it enables us to seem to see some sense and meaning in the nature of things, without which our own lives would have no meaning and make no sense. We believe that human brotherhood, if not a genetic fact, is certainly a metaphorical goal worth working toward and living for. To a large extent we live by metaphors. We might as well live by friendly ones.

There's nothing wrong with living by belief in the metaphor of human brotherhood, even if it seldom works out in practice. We don't arrive at our beliefs by logical analysis or scientific investigation but by personal predilection. We believe what we choose to believe, and we choose according to our nature and nurture: our physiology, our upbringing, our chance experiences, the things that have happened to us, the effects of wind and rain and sun and indoor air, the light reflected from walls outdoors and indoors, the textures of our clothes, the food we have eaten, the warmth or coldness in people's eyes, the things we have heard people say, the tones of their voices, the other sounds in the air, the feel of sand and grass and mud and concrete and asphalt hot and warm and cool and cold and wet and damp and dry on our bare feet, the feel of comfortable and uncomfortable shoes, the unanalyzable totality of our experience, outer and inner. Such are the real sources of our view of human nature. There are of course facts and statistics and Biblical quotations or other wise sayings to support every known view of human nature; from those that are available to us, we choose according to our personal predilections.

This doesn't mean that all beliefs about human nature are equally valid or invalid. Some are pleasanter than others, merely as beliefs to live with; some, moreover, have pleasanter effects on the lives of other people. Look at the faces of libertarians and authoritarians, and you'll see that libertarians are pleasanter people, and—other things being equal—live more pleasantly with themselves and with others. Libertarians tend to be spontaneously and disinterestedly friendly; authoritarians tend to be spontaneously and disinterestedly unfriendly; libertarians instinctively want to help people, or at least leave them alone and not exploit or abuse them; authoritarians instinctively want to exploit or abuse them. We libertarians are frequently deceived; but authoritarians frequently deceive themselves. To trust everybody is doubtless foolish; but to distrust everybody is even more foolish—it is to be even more disastrously ignorant of the way people can be. Even if the authoritarians were in general right, they would still be foolish—because, as Plato observed some time ago, it is better to be deceived by our friends than not to trust them. What is a person who doesn't trust his friends?

The libertarian attitude is by no means blind to the difficulties of living in a world where there are many authoritarians; but we must always be on guard against over-enthusiasm, and against the temptation of seemingly easy solutions. Leopold Bloom's fatuous dream of human perfection involves among other things "esperanto the universal brotherhood." That is the dream of the Tower of Babel: if only we all spoke the same language—if only we understood each other!—we could work our way to Heaven together. At the very least, we would all recognize each other as brothers and sisters, and regard each other with familial affection.

Such metaphors do harm inasmuch as they delude us with unrealizable hopes and divert us from doing the limited but practical things we might do to make life not perfect but somewhat pleasanter. With our eyes full of dreams, we don't see the most obvious facts: e.g., that people who speak the same language, and perfectly understand each other's words, don't necessarily share the same values or presuppositions; that others, who converse with difficulty through a language barrier, may discover that they do share the same values and presuppositions; that the discovery of what they have in common doesn't make them brothers and sisters and doesn't have to in order for them to enjoy each other's company—that they may enjoy their difference of culture as much as their community of feeling; and that, contrariwise, people who are in fact brothers and sisters don't necessarily therefore love each other. Cain and Abel didn't love each other; Jacob and Esau didn't love each other; Romulus and Remus didn't love each other; the Emperor Commodus not only raped his sisters but enjoyed looking on while others, at his invitation, raped them—how's that for brotherly love?—and the famous case of Mark Antony and Octavius Caesar indicates that brothers-in-law not only don't necessarily regard each other with fraternal affection but may not even be able to work together as political allies. History and literature alike are full of battling brothers, all subsumed in Shem and Shaun, the hellish twins of *Finnegans Wake*. Nevertheless we assume that since all men are brothers they should naturally love each other. This assumption involves not only the delusion of taking a metaphor literally but also a kind of inverted racism: the assumption that the human race is genetically homogeneous, and that whereas it might be all right to hate other races—if there were any, haha—it is not all right to hate one's own, the good old human race. This fatuous inverted racism is, to be sure, benign rather than malignant; but it is just as irresponsibly fanciful as the malignant kind.

We don't need any such stupid metaphor as that. Human heterogeneity is plain to see. What we need is not to pretend that we are all alike but to work out ways of living with our individual differences, genetic as well as cultural, and using them in whatever positive ways we can. This requires us to recognize that we have a great deal in common as individuals: because what makes us human—what constitutes our common humanity or human nature—is neither genetic nor cultural homogeneity but the presence of a few traits that all individual human beings share. If you prick us we bleed, if you kill us we die, if you insult us we resent it, if we are well fed we are better off than if we are underfed, if we have some knowledge or skill that society needs and values we are better off than if we haven't, if we are permitted to develop our individual capacities we are better off than if we are not, and high capacity is a quality of individuals, not of races, classes, religions, professions or regions. Facts of this kind make us all brothers and sisters; facts of this kind afford us a basis for working together for our mutual benefit.

They can also afford us a solid basis for judging societies and their governments. We don't have to catch the contagious disease of relativism, the servile notion that whatever is is right. Taking as a standard of value the welfare of individual human beings—the effects of ideas, policies and actions on individual people—we can easily establish objective criteria—facts that are facts everywhere and at all times—by which we can decide that one society is better than another. Here are some. They are so obvious that we frequently leave them out of account and get in trouble.

1. *It is better to be alive than dead.* I know, I know. Don't talk to me about suicide, euthanasia, or Swift's Struldbrugs. Now and then there are intolerable circumstances that are or at least seem to be worse than death. But such circumstances are by definition unfortunate. Nobody doubts that they are unfortunate. They are also rare. Otherwise suicide would not be rare. Death is at best negative. The overwhelming majority of people will put up with a great deal of grief and pain rather than die: life, even under bad conditions, is by overwhelming human agreement worth living. Therefore, we can say that a society is better or worse in proportion to the average life expectancy of its people at birth. In

the United States the average life expectancy at birth has risen from 47.3 years in 1900 to 72 years in 1974; we can therefore say that at least in this respect the conditions of American life were better in 1974 than in 1900. Such bad things as infant mortality, industrial accidents per thousand workers, unhealthy working conditions, etc., have declined, frequently against the pious opposition of those who said it would be immoral to spend money for such purposes; and such good things as life-saving medicines, indoor plumbing, etc., have increased. At least in these respects—at least in terms of such demonstrable facts—we can say that the American society is better than it used to be, and probably better than any other society now going. Those who argue to the contrary are careful to avoid mere plain demonstrable facts; they speak in metaphors and abstractions, they give us pretty romantic pictures out of Disneyland. Ron Ziegler worked for Disneyland before he went to work for Nixon. His new job was to attack the patriotism of reporters who wanted facts. The Russians and the Chinese also have their Zieglers.

Of course improvements in the conditions of life are not evenly distributed: in every country the life expectancy of the poor is considerably less than that of the middle class, and that of the middle class is somewhat less than that of the rich—so that in a very real sense we can say that it is possible to buy life with money. A society in which people have more money for buying life—whether through adequate personal incomes or through adequately funded social medicine and safety programs—is better than one in which they have less. We often forget that physical life—the longest possible and healthiest possible life for the greatest possible number—is the basis of any real human decency. What do I mean by "real"? I mean that such amenities of life as are bought by the misery of others are acceptable only by those who either consent to such misery or delude themselves with the notion that it isn't misery.

The alleged decency of such people is either a lie or a delusion. Therefore: the longest possible and healthiest possible life, and the peacefullest and pleasantest possible life, for the greatest possible number of individual human beings. That is our standard. It isn't possible to do much for the dead. There is no art or science or love or sport or happiness or good living in the grave.

Of course I am aware that the world population is outrunning the food supply. I am also aware that every major country in the world spends more money for missiles, bombs, tanks, mines and machine guns than for agricultural research, and that most of the pious moralists who oppose birth control have no record of comparably active opposition to war and genocide. The Rev. Thomas R. Malthus (1766–1834) said that war and famine become inevitable whenever the population outruns the food supply, and that we must accept them patiently, or else lead celibate lives, because the only alternative is "vice"—i.e., birth control—which is morally unacceptable. He didn't find war, famine or the horrors of celibacy morally unacceptable. This is known as Malthus's Law. Or should we say Malthus's Law and Order? In any case, it has many advocates now: people who urge us to be "practical" and accept the idea that sooner or later the military game planners of one country or another will initiate the blowing up of the human race, and meanwhile to live in such a way as to let it be done by our own game planners rather than any others. By comparison with such craziness, the dream of human brotherhood seems, if not realistic, at least not criminally insane. I therefore propose, as a first step toward giving the term "human brotherhood" some factual substance and practical application, that we all, individually and in groups, advocate before all our legislative bodies, local, state, national and international, the repeal of Malthus's Law. Specifically, that we advocate, in particular concrete ways, with details, a major reordering of our financial priorities; as that reordering occurs, the moral priorities will reorder themselves accordingly. Our lawmakers and administrators do count votes. That is their chief standard of moral value. Our proposals need not be identical, or even similar; but if each were a concrete proposal based on accurate information—to the extent that there is accurate information—and if they all pointed in the same general direction—more money for life, less for death—the message would get through.

How's that for fatuous? What a dream! It would be militarily suicidal for any major country to set out on such a course all alone. Such a major change of direction would be feasible only as an international undertaking; and everybody knows that the purpose of international arms limitations talks is to enable militarists to help each other get more money from their respective governments. Nevertheless, we have to keep thinking in these terms if we are ever to generate enough pressure for change. The mere volume of voices sometimes counts for something.

If it seems hardly serious to think in this way, the grown men who play international chicken with nuclear missiles, solemnly calculating with their aides how many "megadeaths" (i.e., millions of deaths) would be "acceptable," as if they was fidgerin' out how many more marbles they could afford to lose, are hardly qualified to say so; if shifting large sums of money from such games to productive uses (which at the very least would be less inflationary) is an unrealizable dream (albeit a saner dream than the nightmare we are now realizing), then there is no hope for us. But, like the judge in the Scopes trial, we are entitled to hope that we are less stupid than we seem.

2. *In addition to mere outward physical life, we human beings need conditions that make possible the development of our inner life.* I am an animal, but I am not an automaton moved

by reflexes alone and therefore subject to conditioning and manipulation without limit. I have possibilities, however limited, of self-determination. There once was a learned D. Phil. who didn't believe in free will; said a bright Ph.D., "As for me, I am free"; thus the two asses turned the old mill. Nevertheless, when I said earlier that we believe what we choose to believe, that statement was not negated by the statement immediately following, that we choose according to our nature and nurture. The old riddle, "Can we will not to will what we will?" is a question that begs itself. Our nature and nurture are not fixed and finished; they are processes of continuing development. I am what I am, to be sure, but only for the moment; for I am continuously moving and becoming. I do have the power to change my mind. I change it all the time. I change it effectively, in action. By so doing, I change my nature. I am what I do, and I do what I choose to do—the choices are often hard, but no choice is ever compulsory. When I act, I thereby choose to be the kind of person who acts in that way; and in a lifetime of choices of action I become what I choose to become. Sartre was right: after the age of thirty—or forty—I forget—every man is responsible for his own face, but he is not necessarily stuck with its present expression. He can change it, and be responsible for the changes it continues to undergo. As Sartre put it, he is "condemned to be free."

But this existential freedom is subjective, not objective. It enables me—Sartre says it condemns me—to choose to be the kind of person I will be in any situation, either *(a)* by accepting the situation, adjusting to it, conforming to it, or *(b)* by struggling against it, trying to change it, asserting my own values, my own self, against it, or *(c)* by transcending it, through stoicism or mysticism or romantic hope. So far, so good; but subjective freedom doesn't change the objective situation: it doesn't emancipate me from slavery, for example, or from the atmosphere of Sinclair Lewis's

Zenith or the Lynds' Middletown or James Baldwin's Harlem or Sherwood Anderson's Winesburg or Nathanael West's Hollywood—and a person born in such a situation may never have an inkling of the possibilities of action or value that others take for granted. Stephen Sargent Visher's classic investigation, *Geography of American Notables: A Statistical Study of Birthplaces, Training, Distribution: An Effort to Evaluate Various Environmental Factors* (Bloomington, Ind.: Indiana University Studies, No. 79, June 1928), "deals," as he says, "with various sorts of notables, especially the scientists selected by their fellow scientists as especially meritorious (designated by an asterisk in Cattell's *American Men of Science, a Biographical Dictionary*) and of the people sketched in *Who's Who in America.*" His figures are out of date, but his principles are still valid, and the evidence of his maps and tables of figures is clear: a person who wants to make an original contribution to scientific knowledge or be otherwise notable should arrange to be born a boy rather than a girl, white rather than black, in a city rather than on a farm, in an economically prosperous region rather than a poor one, to parents of the professional class, and should by all means go to a top university and do graduate work with a major scholar: because a white boy baby born in Boston or New York or Chicago and educated at Harvard or Johns Hopkins or Columbia does seem to have a somewhat better chance than a black girl baby born in rural Mississippi. Visher observed that the Southern states, whose *white* population (emphasis his) far exceeded that of California, produced far fewer notable people. These facts and others like them indicate another standard by which we can judge societies and their governments: the opportunities they afford us to develop our capacities.

3. *Finally, there is the standard of political freedom.* In a society where there is only one employer, and where moreover there is only one political party, and where moreover the press is responsible to the government

that owns it and the party that staffs it, anybody who has an unorthodox idea and dares to express it may very well find himself or herself out in the street pushing a broom, or in jail, or in a mental hospital; and any artist whose vision doesn't conform to the official vision—the vision that is expressed by the fiction of Mikhail Sholokhov in Russia and José María Gironella in Spain, by the paintings of Norman Rockwell in America, and by official sculpture everywhere—O Pioneers! O Justice! O Agriculture! O Physical Ed! O Lenin! O Mao! O Franco! O Admiral Nelson! O Robert Fulton!—the kind of statue of which Joyce said, "He's saying, 'When I was a boy, the manure pile was that high' "—any artist who wants to do something better than official art is liable to be called degenerate and get in trouble accordingly.

If the term "human brotherhood" means anything concrete and specific, it means something of the kind implied in these standards by which we can judge societies and governments: the welfare of individual people living in society: health and long life, fair opportunities for the development of our capacities, and the freedom to express our personal vision. Otherwise it is an empty metaphor.

10 Prejudice and Literature

PREJUDICE, a prejudgement, an ill opinion formed beforehand.—Walter W. Skeat, *An Etymological Dictionary of the English Language.*

Overt hostility or habitual condescension or discourtesy, arising from prejudice conscious or unconscious, is easy enough to understand, and (on the level of manners) easy enough to deal with; but sometimes, because of social myths that are never articulated but are nevertheless accepted as if they were facts of nature—if only because they are not articulated —the most courteous, most liberal, most humane and gentle people injure others without intending to and without knowing it. Can there be an unintentional enmity? In terms of the practical effects of an unconscious attitude, yes.

Since we reveal our unconscious attitudes in our writing as well as in our speech and behavior, can the fact of an unintentional enmity give us a standard for literary judgment? If so, can the fact of intentional enmity consciously expressed give us a standard for literary judgment?

Literary judgment? . . . I am aware of all the objections, I have stated them myself and will continue to state them. But prejudice tends to disable a writer *as writer,* because it is in its very nature and inevitable expression vulgar.

It is vulgar because it is not personal. Nobody decides, personally, individually, alone, that he dislikes or distrusts or despises a whole race or sex or religion or nation. That is an attitude he picks up from the community or group he lives in. It has nothing to do with personal experience. I grew up in the racially homogeneous white half of a Southern city, where everybody was named Smith or Jones or Robinson—a community that prided itself on being "Anglo-Saxon," and where a name like Bertolucci or Caponetti would have been good for a fit of laughter—and I can tell you that in those pre-television days there were children who had never seen an Italian or even a picture of one, but who grew up believing that dagoes was lowdown. In the third grade a Greek boy joined our class. "Is a Greek the same thing as a dago?" asked one of the children. "Yes," said the teacher. I can also tell you that there are people much more sophisticated, North and South, who (not necessarily knowing a Jew when they see one) have told me, a Jew, that they disliked Jews. "Can you tell a Jew when you see one?" I have asked, and the answer is always to this cliché effect: "Yes. There's something about them." I have said, "Maybe it's their names. Rabinowitz. Moses." And they have said, "No. I'm not prejudiced against them. But they *are* selfish and they *are* pushy and they *are* dishonest." One, a highly literate historian who should have known better, said, "But they *are* Christ-killers." And when I have then informed such people that they were talking to a Jew, they have always tried to assure me that of course they didn't really mean it, or that they were joking, or that I was different, or that some of their best friends . . . .

A writer whose perception of people is thrown off by such acquired vulgarity of mind is inevitably damaged, *as a writer,* whenever he expresses it.

Of course vulgarity is acquired. We are not born vulgar. That tendency is not congenital but habitual. It is not a matter either of violating rules or of conforming to them; it is a matter of the way in which we violate them or conform to them; it is a group style, acquired by imitation as unconsciously as we acquire our regional or class pronunciation: an unimaginative automatism, a taking of metaphors and folk tales literally, a humorlessness, a lack of ease and freedom.

But since it involves a defect of perception, it is not relative but absolute. Vulgarity is absolute. In behavior it is not necessarily a breach of etiquette, which differs from place to place and changes from time to time, but a lack of courtesy, which is a quality of the soul—the soul itself being a habitual disposition.

In attitude and belief it is not necessarily a matter of being wrong about matters of fact—i.e., of being uninformed or misinformed or simply fallible; it is rather a matter of being infallible: of being unable to conceive. that any other attitude or belief is possible except as an aberration or a perversity. It is a defensive narrowness of vision. We avoid seeing what nobody else sees. We don't dare to violate the etiquette of the local infallibles—an etiquette that commands not only our speech but also our feelings. We choose to be timid through and through.

In literature it is an invariable use of the cliché conception, the cliché device, the cliché metaphor, the cliché pattern or conclusion. This may consist either in an automatic following of academic or commercial models or in an automatic following of the currently fashionable new direction. Such literary vulgarity is the inevitable result of a writer's expressing his intellectual vulgarity, whatever this may be.

There is no intellectual vulgarity more disabling to a writer than a racial or religious or national or social or sexual prejudice, be it positive or negative.
Sentimentality throws off our judgment; ill will throws it off at least as much. The tendency to regard people not as individuals but as typical specimens makes it difficult or impossible to see them in their uniqueness and unpredictability; it keeps us from seeing the personal qualities of the people around us and the nuances of their relations with each other and with ourselves, and inclines us to see phantoms or devils: subhuman beings who aren't there at all. When prejudiced whites look at Ralph Ellison they don't see him, they see a nigger; Henry Adams, without having read Bergson, called him a fly in the milk of philosophy; all members of groups that are objects of prejudice are similarly invisible to prejudiced eyes; and when a writer misconceives the people around him he is disabled indeed. To whatever extent he writes under the influence of a vulgar delusion, his work is cheapened. Let us observe some cases, minor and major: the inadvertent offenders Valery Larbaud, James Joyce and Charles Lamb, the doubtful case of Charles Dickens, and the deliberate offenders T. S. Eliot, Ezra Pound and William Shakespeare. The result in each case is literary vulgarity. This conclusion seems to me so simple and obvious that I feel some embarrassment in presenting it, and do so only because I have not seen it or heard it before.

INADVERTENT OFFENDERS

Larbaud

"Vulgarity" is not a word that occurs to us in connection with Valery Larbaud. Unlike some other men who inherit millions, and who devote their lives to accumulating more millions, or to politics or sport or the social game, Larbaud devoted his to literature, and made highly readable contributions—as critic, translator, publicist, parodist, essayist, and writer of stories—that seem to me too little appreciated. Though he wrote a great deal, including some illuminating appreciations of Irish, English and American writers, not one of his works is now in print in English; to most readers of English he is either the author of one sentence—"With *Ulysses* Ireland makes a triumphant and sensational re-entrance into high European literature"—or of nothing; that is a minor misfortune, because by overlooking him we miss some very pleasant minor pleasures. His fresh, original critical intelligence, his easy, unaffected, humorous urbanity, his unsentimental sentiment, his tincture of poetry, gave everything he wrote the quality of fine conversation. From time to time I dip into the Pléïade one-volume selection, as I dip into Bemelmans or Nabokov or Isaac Bashevis Singer, always with pleasure.

I was therefore dismayed recently when my eye, looking for another passage in another story, fell on a passage in "Mon Plus Secret Conseil" at which women who are sensitive to their situation as women can justly take offense. Having had that shock, for a time I enjoyed him less easily, more warily, as if it were shameful even to enjoy his prose, given the unconscious attitude revealed by that passage. That experience was the occasion of this chapter.

"Mon Plus Secret Conseil," like several other fictions of Larbaud's, is an autobiographical fantasy. And like *Ulysses,* it is partly narrated by the author, partly drawn from the stream of consciousness of the central character: one Lucas Letheil, a young man who has recently come into a large fortune, who regards poets as the noblest of all beings, who intends to develop his own poetic gifts, who wants to live in a manner worthy of his intelligence, his sensibility and his high calling—or, as he puts it, "my high birth"—but who through lack of experience makes ludicrous mistakes. In the passage my eye fell on, this innocent Des Esseintes is making up his mind to run away from his current mistress, who though beautiful is compulsively quarrelsome and has subjected him to increasingly violent storms, in private and in public, at shorter and shorter intervals. He has asked the advice of his friend Gustave; Gustave has advised him not to be hasty, since it isn't every man who has as mistress the divorced wife of a former Cabinet minister. "Poor Gustave," Lucas thinks, ". . . she is for him what a woman would be for me if she had been the mistress of a great poet."

The two young men, though their values are certainly different, are at one in assuming that a woman is little or nothing more than a reflection of a man—the Sidney's-sister-Pembroke's-mother fallacy. That vulgar assumption has done a great deal of harm to women. (I realize that I am being humorless; I realize also that one of the tactics of humorless prejudice is to throw an insult in your face and then say, "Have you no sense of humor?") To be sure, the assumption is Lucas', not necessarily Larbaud's; and to be sure, Larbaud's auctorial smile is quite evident; nevertheless, Lucas' prevailing tone is much like that of all of Larbaud's personae, and there is every reason to believe that Larbaud found them amiable albeit absurd or even grotesque representations of himself. He seems as unaware as Lucas and his mistress that there is any cause for her seemingly gratuitous rage. He is not interested in her rage or in its conceivable causes, but only in Lucas' reactions to it.

Part of my shock on reading the passage this time was due to the realization that it had not shocked me before. Being a Jew, I have always been sensitive ("over-sensitive," as the revealing cliché goes) to the slightest indications not only of anti-Semitism but of any racial, religious, class, cultural or national prejudice: Lamb's "Imperfect Sympathies" shocked me the first time I read it, by its bland unembarrassed confession of an irrational dislike not only of Jews but also of Scots,

Blacks and Quakers, and I grew up in the South defiantly bearing the stigma "nigger-lover"; but the first time I read that passage of Larbaud's, in 1965, it seemed to me nothing more or less than witty. At that time I was not aware that there was such a thing as sexual prejudice.

Nor was Larbaud aware of it, evidently. He despised racial, religious, cultural and national prejudices as he despised all other manifestations of vulgarity; and there is no doubt in my mind that if he had been aware of the existence of sexual prejudice he would have despised it. He was not a man of ill will or of insufficient self-esteem: he had no need to take pride in belonging to one race rather than another, or to one sex rather than the other. He simply accepted the position of women as he accepted the fact that rivers flow downhill. There had been too little agitation to make him—or me—aware that it was not inherent in nature. We were both guilty of a vulgar attitude toward women, a vulgar misconception of women: a vulgar unthinking assumption that they are not quite fully human.

Lucas is, to be sure, a caricature of Larbaud, but a friendly caricature; if his misconception of the nature of women reflects a misconception by Larbaud, it reflects a failure of insight; if it doesn't reflect a misconception by Larbaud, Larbaud's failure to make this clear is a failure of technique. In either case, it is a failure of art: a literary failure. In the absence of ill will, I am not sure we can call it a moral failure; but the intellectual requirements of literature are higher than those of morality.

Joyce

Larbaud's master Joyce also—the intelligence, energy and spirit of Harriet Weaver, Sylvia Beach, Adrienne Monnier, Dora Marsden, Margaret Anderson, Jane Heap, Maria Jolas, Mary Colum and Caresse Crosby notwithstanding—accepted the traditional view that women were creatures of earth, impulse and convention, swinging mindless between id and super-ego. This is clear in his famous description of the "Penelope" chapter of *Ulysses:*

> It begins and ends with the female word *yes.* It turns like the huge earth ball slowly surely and evenly, round and round spinning, its 4 cardinal points being the female breasts, arse, womb and cunt expressed by the words *because, bottom* (in all uses bottom button, bottom of the class, bottom of the sea, bottom of his heart), *woman, yes.* Though probably more obscene than any preceding episode it seems to me perfectly sane full amoral fertilisable untrustworthy engaging shrewd limited prudent indifferent *Weib. Ich bin der Fleisch der stets bejaht.* [Quoted in Richard Ellmann, *James Joyce,* pp. 516–17. There are three other versions, all slightly different: one by Ellmann in *Ulysses on the Liffey,* p. 164, one by Frank Budgen in *Letters of James Joyce,* I, 170, and one by Budgen in *James Joyce and the Making of Ulysses,* pp. 262–63.]

Whatever the exact wording may be, this passage in each of its four versions indicates that "Penelope" takes us into the mind of a female, innocent of all the refinements of perception male human beings have developed in some five thousand years of civilization. Molly Bloom and Anna Livia Plurabelle sum up all of Joyce's women, not one of whom has any germ of intellect. Perhaps it is worth noting that the German *Weib* is neuter. Why else would the polyglot Joyce have chosen it from among all the words he knew for woman, of which at least one or two must have been feminine? Molly is Aristotelian matter waiting to be fertilized by the imposition of form.

How's that for far-fetched? It seems far-fetched to me. The trouble with *Ulysses* is that it lends itself to, and tempts us into, far-fetched readings. Certainly in this case Joyce himself has imposed form on Molly's primitive matter. Diane Tolomeo's brilliant article "The Final Octagon of 'Ulysses'" (*James Joyce Quarterly*, X, no. 4 [summer 1973], 439–54) demonstrates that the eight sentences of "Penelope" do indeed form a circle or rather a capital U, the eighth sentence reversing and mirroring the first, the seventh reversing and mirroring the second, etc., so that Molly's soliloquy, which we used to think was formless, turns out to be perhaps the most tightly organized chapter in the second most tightly organized of all novels (*Finnegans Wake* being the firstmost).[1]

In this case can we say that Joyce's acceptance of the cliché view of women leads him into a literary failure? Certainly the chapter itself is a consummate piece of construction. But yes, we can say that even in this case there is a failure of insight, and that in a novel a failure of insight is a failure of art. We can say this even while we rejoice in the brilliance of the construction, the language, the psychology, the valid insights. My wife says, "Joyce's vision of Woman doesn't include a head. That's a very bad oversight. That's what we've been fighting."

Lamb

Where there is good will, as with Joyce and Larbaud, such failures of insight are unfortunate astigmatisms; where there is ill will, they are the self-inflicted

[1] My son, Jonathan, writes, "Did Tolomeo discuss—has anybody discussed—Joyce's description of 'Penelope' in terms of a synthesis of antitheses?—i.e.,
Woman is—
sane but amoral
full but fertilisable
untrustworthy but engaging
shrewd but limited
prudent but indifferent
—*Weib* as the resolution of all oxymora? In that case Joyce is not imposing form on Molly's primitive matter simply for the sake of literary technique but rather for the sake of exemplifying his supra-literary theory of humanity."

hallucinations of writers who, as Sartre would say, have chosen to be irrational. But there are cases where there is no ill will, merely a lack of good will, or perhaps of imagination. Charles Lamb is such a case. In "Imperfect Sympathies" he *knows* that he is having hallucinations, but he finds them rather fun, and doubtless charming to others. He confesses his irrational dislikes as weaknesses, failings, personal imperfections, of little or no consequence, analogous to being unable to tie a cravat smoothly (oh, dear) or leaving one's umbrella in the coffee house (oh, *dear!*). He evidently expects his readers to view them with the same amused tolerance that he does, if not with outright sympathy; whatever his expectation may be, in the deprecatory self-centeredness that is the signature of his presence in "Imperfect Sympathies" as elsewhere, he seems not to realize that his attitude does harm to others. He doesn't wish us any harm; his dislike is not aggressive; to call it ill will would be to exaggerate and falsify it; his policy is live and let live, separately but . . . well, separately. He wishes we were elsewhere. He wishes we would all just go away. He doesn't actually wish we didn't exist: he doesn't permit himself to have murderous thoughts—no such thing would ever occur to him—the trouble is, he just hasn't thought about the subject very much, and it shows. In "Imperfect Sympathies" he has for once undertaken a subject too big for his small talent; as a result, he is not charming, as elsewhere, but simply ignorant, fatuous and presumptuous. In what is intended to be an urbane essay, these are literary faults. The fact that his approving audience was equally ignorant, fatuous and presumptuous doesn't make him less so.

A DOUBTFUL CASE

Dickens

George Orwell denies that the creator of Fagin (1838) was anti-Semitic. That is to define anti-Semitism narrowly indeed. Without quite saying so, he implies that Fagin was probably drawn from life and that the choice of model was not influenced by any vulgar preconception. That is to overlook the cliché nature of the portrait. Remarking on Dickens's freedom from xenophobia, Orwell says:

> It is perhaps more significant that he shows no prejudice against Jews. It is true that he takes it for granted (*Oliver Twist* and *Great Expectations*) that a receiver of stolen goods will be a Jew, which at the time was probably justified. But the "Jew joke," endemic in English literature until the rise of Hitler, does not appear in his books, and in *Our Mutual Friend* he makes a pious though not very convincing attempt to stand up for Jews. ["Charles Dickens," in *The Collected Essays, Journalism and Letters of George Orwell*, ed. Sonia Orwell and Ian Angus (4 vols., New York: Harcourt, Brace & World, 1968), I, 433.]

The exculpation seems to me too little qualified. I think a more nearly accurate statement would be that Dickens was anti-Semitic in the same way that a child is anti-Semitic, believing as a matter of course what he was taught at home and in Sunday school.

Dickens himself, in a letter to Mrs. Eliza Davis, a Jewish woman who protested that the portrayal of Fagin did "a great wrong" to all Jews, denied the charge:

> Fagin, in *Oliver Twist,* is a Jew, because it unfortunately was true of the time to which the story refers, that that class of criminal almost invariably *was* a Jew. But surely no sensible man or woman of your persuasion can fail to observe—firstly—that all the rest of the wicked dramatis personae are Christians; and, secondly, that he is called "the Jew," not because of his religion, but because of his race. . . . I have no feeling towards the Jewish people but a friendly one.

. . . And in my *Child's History of England* I have lost no opportunity of setting forth their cruel persecution in old times. [Quoted in Montagu Frank Modder, *The Jew in the Literature of England* (Jewish Publication Society of America, 1939; rpt. Meridian Books, 1960), p. 220.]

That letter was written July 10, 1863. But between 1838 and 1863 the climate had changed. Let me merely recall the chronology of the change, without asserting any necessary connection between it and Dickens's change of tone. In 1837 Benjamin Disraeli, a baptized Anglican, had been elected to Parliament, but his maiden speech was howled down, and after making several starts he broke it off with the statement, "the time will come when you will hear me!" In 1847, 1850 and 1853, unconverted Jews had been elected to Parliament, but could not be seated because they could not take the oath "on the true faith of a Christian"; in 1858, after having been introduced and defeated for twenty-nine consecutive years, the Jewish Emancipation Bill was passed, and Baron Rothschild, having been elected, was permitted to take the oath as a member of the House of Commons with the alternative words, "So help me, Jehovah!" (Modder, pp. 160–63; Cecil Roth, *A History of the Jews,* [rev. ed., New York: Schocken Books, 1970], pp. 332–33.)

In *Our Mutual Friend* (1863), Dickens tried to make amends for *Oliver Twist* by portraying a "good" Jew, "the gentle Mr. Riah." But Mr. Riah is too gentle to be a believable human being, and on March 1, 1867, Dickens felt impelled to asseverate to Mrs. Davis his "real regard" for the Jews, "a people to whom I would not wilfully have given an offence or done an injustice for any worldly consideration." (Modder, p. 221.)

Having slapped Mrs. Davis in the face, he was sincerely puzzled as to why she took offense, and tried to assure her that he hadn't meant any harm. Such are the effects of unquestioned custom.

My wife points out that in roughly the first half of *Oliver Twist* Dickens treats Fagin differently from the other characters, however villainous, in that he seldom uses his name, referring to him usually as "the Jew," but that in the second half he usually calls him "Fagin" and seldom "the Jew." She is right. I open the 1941 Dodd, Mead edition casually to seven pairs of facing pages where Fagin appears. On pp. 80–81 he is "the Jew" eleven times, "Fagin" once, and "the old gentleman" once; on pp. 186–87 he is "the Jew" eight times and "Fagin" once; on pp. 252–53 he is "the Jew" ten times and "Fagin" twice, one of these two occasions being when he is directly addressed by Monks; but on pp. 380–81 he is "the Jew" twice, "the wary old Jew" once, and "Fagin" six times, including once when he refers to himself as "poor ould Fagin"; on pp. 428–29 he is "the Jew" once, "Mr. Fagin" once, and "Fagin" seven times; and on pp. 534–35, when he is being led to the gallows, he is only "Fagin"—six times.

Such are perhaps the effects of serial publication, though Dickens's letters for 1837–38, the period of serialization, which I have consulted, don't show any answers to complaints or objections; perhaps Dickens felt that the generic term had lost some of its force through iteration and would begin to bore the readers; or perhaps it had begun to bore him; or perhaps it was no longer necessary for the purpose of identification; or perhaps by unconscious design Fagin was "the Jew" when he was rising and "Fagin" when he was falling; in any case, by page 380 the phrase "the Jew" had already done its damage.[2] I invite my readers, mutatis mutandis,

[2] Jonathan again: "Disregarding such formulations as 'Mr. Fagin,' I arrange your citations as follows:

	First half	Second half
'Fagin'	4 citations	19
'The Jew'	29	4

Having done so, I perform an old reliable statistical manipulation known as the chi-square test, which tangles all these figures chiasmatically up, top right and bottom left, top left and bottom right,

to consider the effects of having a completely evil character referred to repeatedly as "the American," or "the Irishman," or "the German," or "the Catholic," or "the Methodist," in a society where Americans or Irish or Germans or Catholics or Methodists were in legal fact second-class citizens and were commonly regarded as evil; and to consider what effect an unbelievably good and gentle American or Irish or German or Catholic or Methodist character could have after their legal disabilities had begun to be removed. (Not until 1871 were any but Anglicans admitted to British universities [Winston Churchill, *A History of the English Speaking Peoples* (4 vols., New York: Dodd, Mead, 1956–58), IV, 287–88].)[3]

and reduces them all to a single naked number. The bigger that number is, the greater the probability that the difference you're examining is real. In this particular case, the chi-square value is 24.987, which is, as chi-square values go, huge; and that means that if your sample is at all representative of the tendency in the whole book, there's almost no chance at all that Dickens's switch from 'the Jew' to 'Fagin' was a random thing. Now in your next paragraph you attempt to explain what happened, but it occurs to me that you're dealing with a change so large that merely literary explanations are probably insufficient. 1838 was the year of the People's Charter; could that have had anything to do with it?"

[3] And again: "This is an oversimplification. Subscription to the Thirty-Nine Articles was a requirement for admission to Oxford but only for graduation from Cambridge; therefore, some non-Anglicans went through Cambridge and got everything but the degree. I wonder how Dickens's readers viewed the growth of official tolerance, and I think they may have been optimistic about it. After all, the universities had sunk to their lowest depths in the eighteenth century, with tradition stagnant, frozen; and their anti-Catholic bias, like the rest of their way of life, must have seemed anachronistic by Dickens's time. The Catholic Emancipation Act had after all been passed in 1829, the year the Jewish Emancipation Act was first introduced. Did Dickens's readers—the same middle class that shared Trollope's and Gilbert's amused contempt for the controversy surrounding the Oxford Movement—look on Fagin as mostly a reminder of the bad old days? Official tolerance, a mild, assimilating thing—Be a Jew in the house and a man in the street—is an anti-Semitic thing too, if you want to use that adjective; but it's an anti-Semitism of the eighteenth- and nineteenth-century kind, not of the twentieth. It survives today in the democratic secular state of Palestine, where Jew, Christian and Moslem

Fagin is more believable than Mr. Riah not because he is more truly observed or more accurately drawn but because he has the superior vividness of the grotesque— as a literary creation he is superior to Mr. Riah in the same way that Squire Western is superior to Squire Allworthy—and as a salable item he is superior for this reason and also because he conforms in every detail to the popular cliché notion of what Jews were. Dickens was the most popular writer of his time because—as many critics have remarked—he had a fine sense of his audience. In Fagin he gave them a variety-theater stage Jew, with the standard red hair, the standard dirtiness, the standard obsequiousness, the standard gloating over a hoard of jewels, the standard readiness to stab a Christian child with a bread knife or break his bones with a club.

Moreover, as my wife points out again, in Oliver Fagin victimizes his natural superior—for Oliver, though he was born in a workhouse and until his tenth year has never heard any but workhouse speech, and though Dickens says explicitly that his education was limited to picking oakum, nevertheless speaks upper-class English, as if it were in his blood. Fagin's other victims and associates, with the exception of Oliver's half-brother Monks, all speak the language of their trade and their "low" neighborhood. Fagin himself sees that Oliver is "not like other boys in the same circumstances" (p. 252). Thus Dickens catered to a social as well as to an ethnic superstition.

Oliver Twist's popularity on the stage matched its popularity as a novel in Dickens's own time, and has

can live in peace provided they're all Arabs, and there it's sinister indeed, concealing all the evil that a willful anachronism can conceal; but at least in the nineteenth century it was not quite the same as the Hitlerian version of anti-Semitism with which you equate it."

I accept all these amendments except the one in the last clause: I don't equate nineteenth-century anti-Semitism with Hitler's, which was much closer to that of the middle ages and the Inquisition.

continued to do so down into our time; and the portrayal of Fagin continues to feed the most vulgar prejudices—in children as well as in their parents. Dickens's disavowals had and have no effect. His primary audience consisting largely of English Christians, its members were not likely to take Mr. Bumble, Bill Sikes, Noah Claypole and the Artful Dodger as typical Christians or typical Englishmen—they were not likely to use the vulgar word "typical" at all in connection with such grotesques; but they did indeed, and do indeed, use it in connection with the Jewish grotesque Fagin, seeing him as "a typical Jew" (a reaction I have heard more than once) because their religious tradition suggests that he is.

Fagin in the condemned cell curses and beats off the "venerable men of his own persuasion" who come to pray with him; Dickens's apologists like to point out that this proves that Dickens didn't regard him as a representative of the Jewish religion; but—as Eliot has suggested—an atheistic Jew is at least as intolerable as any other; and—since the Jews are not a race—to indicate, however inadvertently, that Fagin's characteristics are racial rather than religious is to underscore the vulgarity of the conception.

Let us take Dickens at his word that the conception was not his own, and that he did not undertake the literary representation or permit the dramatic representation of it for any worldly consideration; and let us agree with the many Dickensians who assert that his purpose as a writer was to make the world better by encouraging people to be individually more decent in their attitudes and behavior. Then we are left with the conclusion that in creating Fagin he inadvertently counteracted his purpose. That was a literary inadvertency.

DELIBERATE OFFENDERS

But what shall we say of the unmistakable ill will of
unmistakably major writers? Is the expression of ill will a
literary fault?

Here we must make a distinction.

Ill will against an individual may indeed be irrational,
but it is not so of necessity and in principle; the literary
expression of it, therefore, is not of necessity and in
principle a literary fault. A Dante or a Swift, paying off
personal scores and political scores, may very well be
unfair in some or in many cases, and certainly it takes a
great deal of chutzpah[4] to put one's enemies in Hell; but
in our personal relationships we don't expect to be, and
are not expected to be, completely rational all the time.
We are not Houyhnhnms, we can't be, we wouldn't want
to be. We can give no objectively demonstrable reasons
for our unmotivated likes and dislikes; to pretend to
would be to make a pretension to infallibility. Since no
two of us are identical in all respects, to like one person
better than another is not only natural but inevitable; it
doesn't mean that we are out of touch with reality. But
to dislike in advance people we have never seen or heard
of is to be out of touch with reality. To dislike a whole
race, nation, sex, class or religion, on the gratuitous
assumption that all its members are identical in certain
undesirable ways—the English are humorless, the French
are immoral, the Irish are drunkards, the Jews will do
anything for money, the Blacks are stupid, the Italians
are gangsters, the Americans are arrogant, women are
emotionally unstable—to live in such a simple world is to
lack discrimination, to be lost in abstraction, and
incidentally to assume that we are infallible in our
pre-judgments. To express such childish dogmatism,
such infallible pre-judgment, in a poem or story or play,

---

4 In case anybody wants a translation, the English word is *hubris.*

is to express vulgarity unintentionally. That is a literary fault.

It is terribly easy to sink into abstraction and lose sight of the living people before our eyes. Eliot, Pound and Shakespeare, their genius notwithstanding, have all sometimes expressed vulgarity unintentionally. But their unintended self-revelations have occurred while they were intentionally expressing ill will, or at the very least —and it comes to the same thing—intentionally catering to the ill will of others.

Eliot

Eliot, the complete reactionary, disapproved of liberal education for women. In the "Fresca" section of *The Waste Land,* which he deleted when Pound suggested that his verse was not as good as Pope's (facsimile edition, ed. Valerie Eliot [New York: Harcourt, Brace, Jovanovich, 1971], pp. 23, 27, 127), he mocked it:

> But women intellectual grow dull,
> And lose the mother wit of natural trull.

And in *The Idea of a Christian Society* (London, [Faber & Faber, 1939], pp. 15, 54) he defended the Nazi notion that women's only proper concerns were the children, the kitchen and the church. One thinks of Hannah Arendt and Barbara Tuchman, both of whom would have been denied education, on the double grounds of being women and being Jews, if Eliot's values had prevailed. If, indeed, they had been permitted to live.

After the military defeat of Nazism, overt expressions of racism and anti-Semitism became for the most part unacceptable in polite society, and they have not yet fully regained their former unquestioned respectability; such words as "nigger," "dago" and "kike" seem to have been replaced in polite conversation by such relatively refined words as "shit," "fuck" and "cunt"; at least, let us hope so; in any case, after the defeat, Eliot denied that he was anti-Semitic. "It is a terrible slander on a man," he said (Bernard Bergonzi, *T. S. Eliot* [New York: Macmillan, 1972], pp. 123–24), and "I am a Christian, and therefore I am not an anti-Semite" (Robert Giroux, "A Personal Memoir," in *T. S. Eliot: The Man and His Work,* ed. Allen Tate [New York: Delacorte Press, 1966], p. 341).

In that case, either he was slandering himself or he was not a Christian when he wrote *After Strange Gods,* "Gerontion," "Sweeney Among the Nightingales," "Burbank with a Baedeker, Bleistein with a Cigar," and the insane Bleistein parody of "Phlebas the Phoenician," which he cut out of *The Waste Land* when Pound asked if he thought it added anything (facsimile edition, pp. 119, 130–31). Gerontion's landlord, Bleistein and "Rachel *née* Rabinovitch" are simply verbal equivalents of the ugly cartoon Jews of the right-wing press, a cliché conception as vulgar as that of the stock silk-hatted cigar-smoking pig-faced Bloated Capitalists of the left-wing press. There is no art in these stereotypes, only the naive expression of a vulgar prejudice. Gerontion is annoyed because London is full of foreigners; Eliot is annoyed by the narrator of "Mélange Adultère de Tout," an impudent wandering Jew doing things that Jews should not be permitted to do. (That title, incidentally, smells of Gobineau.)

Likewise, the simian Sweeney of "Sweeney Erect" and "Sweeney Among the Nightingales" was quite evidently inspired by the vulgar cartoon Irishmen of Eliot's childhood and youth, who were always simian; and the title "Sweeney Erect" suggests a vulgar joke mentioned by Thomas F. Gossett, "about the wheelbarrow being the greatest invention of all time because it had been the means of teaching the Irishman to walk on his hind legs" (*Race: The History of an Idea in America* [New York: Schocken Books, 1965], p. 97).

That these unmistakable manifestations of ill will represent Eliot's own view, not that of any narrator or character unrelated to Eliot, is indicated by his lifelong warm personal admiration of the racist Charles Maurras, who deliberately instigated anti-Semitic riots in the streets and anti-intellectual riots in university classrooms; by his explicit advocacy up to 1939 of Maurras' brand of fascism; by his explicit refusal to criticize Maurras' mobs; and by his notorious statements in *After Strange Gods* that the South is to be congratulated on having been "less invaded by foreign races" than the North and that in the good society "reasons of race and religion combine to make any large number of free-thinking Jews undesirable" (*After Strange Gods* [London: Faber & Faber, 1934], pp. 19–20).

This suggestion, which Eliot offered to students at the University of Virginia in 1933, when Hitler was beginning to put into practice as Reichskanzler the policies on the basis of which he had been elected and appointed, and when the Ku Klux Klan was marching in well-attended parades through the streets of Southern capitals, was hardly innocent or inadvertent. For although he quotes as epigraph to the introduction to *Notes towards the Definition of Culture* Lord Acton's statement, "I think our studies ought to be all but purposeless. They want to be pursued with chastity like mathematics," Eliot himself, on page 86 of the same volume (New York: Harcourt, Brace, 1949), says, "There is no species of thinking which can be quite without effect upon action." No man writes such a propaganda tract without at least hoping, however wistfully, that it will have some effect upon action; and when a racist or an anti-Semite who is also a poet puts vulgar expressions of prejudice into his poems, with the evident expectation that they will move his readers as he himself is moved, he is in no position to ask that we ignore them when we judge his performance. Words are not merely musical sounds or typographical configurations; they have meanings and associations of long standing. They direct our lives. Nobody is a bigot for *literary* reasons; if he puts bigotry into his poems, he is writing not only as a poet but also as a bigot. As a matter of abstract theory, this need not have bad literary effects, any more than love has bad literary effects if a lover who is also a poet writes both as poet and as lover. But bigotry and love are not of equal value as materials for personal poetry. We are dealing not with algebraic equations but with revelations of the soul. To express the bigotry of a Tartuffe or a Malvolio is a valid undertaking for a poet; to express one's own—as Eliot does in "Gerontion," the Bleistein poems and the Sweeney poems I have mentioned—is to express one's own intellectual cheapness, shabbiness, *mesquinerie*, vulgarity. It is to write vulgar poetry. This is not to say that all of Eliot's poetry is vulgar, or to dismiss him as no more than a vulgar poet—who could so misconceive the author of the sestina in "The Dry Salvages"? It is merely to observe that he had a streak of vulgarity, and that it cheapened the poems in which he expressed it.

Some critics, with embarrassed or perhaps with sympathetic tact, simply ignore Eliot's vulgar outbursts (e.g., Audrey F. Cahill, *T. S. Eliot and the Human Predicament* [Natal: University of Natal Press, 1967]).

Some critics enthusiastically praise such outbursts (e.g., John Crowe Ransom, writing on "Gerontion" in Allen Tate's *T. S. Eliot: The Man and His Work*). He finds "Gerontion" one of the best of Eliot's poems, and on pp. 140–41 praises, as one of the best of the passages he finds praiseworthy "both as to their substance and as to their rhythms," the passage beginning "And the jew squats on the window sill, the owner."

Some of Eliot's friends have flatly denied that he was anti-Semitic (e.g., Robert Giroux); some, self-defensively slandering many people, have denied that he was more anti-Semitic than any other non-Jew (e.g., Herbert Read);

but such statements have nothing to do with literary criticism. When such evasiveness enters into a work of criticism, it damages that criticism, just as any other fudging of facts would damage it. Roger Kojecky, for example, in *T. S. Eliot's Social Criticism* ([New York: Farrar, Straus and Giroux, 1971], p. 12), is disingenuous:

> It is difficult to construct a convincing case for Eliot's having been an anti-Semite. To hold a racial philosophy of this sort, and to permit a few ambiguities are, after all, different things. The notorious passage in *After Strange Gods* (p. 19) is capable of the interpretation that a community of *orthodox* Jews would be socially 'desirable' because of the strong social bonds established by Jewish solidarity.

It is not capable of any such interpretation. In the first place, anti-Semitism is not a philosophy, any more than xenophobia is a philosophy; even if it were, since we Jews are not a race, it could not be a racial philosophy. In the second place, there is no Jewish solidarity, even among orthodox Jews. In the third place, the notorious passage in *After Strange Gods* is not ambiguous. Kojecky doesn't quote it; this enables him to ignore the clause "reasons of race and religion combine." Since Eliot's stated objection is neither to Jews nor to atheists but only to atheistic Jews, the assumption that he could tolerate Jews if they were not atheists involves unavoidably the assumption that he could tolerate atheists if they were not Jews. Kojecky is hardly a thinker. Nor does he quote or even mention the following passage from a radio talk appended to *The Idea of a Christian Society* ([London: Faber & Faber, 1939], pp. 71–72):

> What is often assumed, and it is a principle that I wish to oppose, is the principle of live-and-let-live. It

is assumed that if the State leaves the Church alone, and to some extent protects it from molestation, then the Church has no right to interfere with the organisation of society, or with the conduct of those who deny its beliefs. It is assumed that any such interference would be the oppression of the majority by a minority. Christians must take a very different view of their duty.

Nothing in all of Eliot's work suggests that he would regard the presence of orthodox Jews as desirable, or that in a country with a Christian majority—by which, he makes it clear, he means a majority of serious church-goers who go with intellectual conviction—he would not want the Church "to interfere . . . with the conduct of those who deny its beliefs." He emphasizes the point that the essential difference between Christians and non-Christians is a matter not of morality but of theology (pp. 46–48). It is for this that he would oppress us non-Anglicans.

Pound

The case of Pound is both easier and more difficult than that of Eliot: easier because he was more open and less hedged about with seeming qualifications in his fascism, racism and anti-Semitism; more difficult because his literary achievement was both greater and less than Eliot's.

As my son Jonathan once put it, Pound was like those colorful Confederate generals who charged picturesquely ahead, leaving their flanks unprotected—Pickett, Beauregard—whereas Eliot was like the less dashing but more effective Union generals—Grant, Sherman. Pound called Eliot "Old Possum," and in 1937 said, "During the past 20 years the chief or average complaint against the almost reverend Eliot has been that he exaggerated his moderations" (*Polite Essays* [London: Faber & Faber], p. 98). Pound had no moderations. William M. Chace, in

The Political Identities of Ezra Pound and T. S. Eliot
(Stanford, Calif.: Stanford University Press, 1973), makes
quite clear the strategic and tactical differences between
Pound's mad viciousness and Eliot's bland
misrepresentations.

The life of Ezra Pound was tragic in the full classic
sense of the word; it was part of the larger tragedy of a
whole era, and, insofar as he welcomed and cooperated
with the forces of evil, he did nothing to try to prevent
that tragedy. Of course poets have never been the
unacknowledged legislators of mankind or the movers
and shakers of the world, and if I could write the laws I
wouldn't care who wrote the ballads. The value of poetry
is not political or social but aesthetic. Certainly in the
twentieth century no poet or critic of poetry has had any
influence at all, as poet or critic, on the course of public
events; but Yeats had some as an Irish Senator,
D'Annunzio had a little as a soldier, Marinetti may have
had some as a sycophant, and Pound did his bit, for
however little it was worth, as a propagandist. His tragic
flaws were an extreme irritability, a romantic love of
distant violence, a vulgar racism, and a vulgar desire to
save the world by propagating The Truth About Money.

For the purposes of this chapter, which is concerned
with literary judgment, only the literary effects of these
flaws matter; his fascism likewise has no other
importance for this chapter, and will therefore be merely
illustrated, not analyzed and compared with other brands
of fascism. The aspects of it that matter for our purposes
are those it shares with all other brands—to say nothing
of the fatuity of drawing subtle ideological distinctions
between one swaggering vulgarian and another.

Pound's friend and sympathetic biographer Noel Stock
says that he was not a fascist—i.e. (!), that he did *not*
recommend the wearing of uniforms, etc. (*The Life of
Ezra Pound* [New York: Pantheon Books, 1970; rpt. Avon
Discus Books, 1974], p. 452); and Pound himself, at his
arraignment, shouted, "I never did believe in Fascism,

God damn it; I am opposed to Fascism" (p. 542). But
that was sophistry or cynicism or madness; Stock admits
that Pound defended fascism in Eliot's *Criterion* and in
The New York World-Telegram in 1933 (p. 408), and in the
London *Morning Post* and the Paris edition of *The New
York Herald-Tribune* in 1934 (p. 420); that in 1935 and
1936 (when Italy was invading Ethiopia) he wrote to
American and British editors many letters "publicly and
privately defending Italy and Fascism" (p. 436); during
all the subsequent years until the end of World War II,
as Stock, a conscientious chronicler, shows in detail, he
was a frequent and valued contributor to fascist
newspapers and magazines, in Germany, Italy, Japan,
England and the United States; if he was opposed to
fascism, he blatantly misrepresented himself until that
afternoon in court. There is no evidence at all that he
ever opposed it. All the evidence is on the other side. In
a pamphlet, *What Is Money For?*, which he wrote in 1938
for Sir Oswald Mosley's British Union of Fascists, Pound
said, "Usury is the cancer of the world, which only the
surgeon's knife of Fascism can cut out of the life of
nations" (Stock, p. 453). Stock says that for America and
he thinks for England Pound favored democracy
improved by the application of "some Fascist ideas" (p.
54); but Chace cites a number of statements in which
Pound urges that democracy be entirely replaced by
fascism, the only cure for the "mongrelization" of
society (pp. 7, 9, 64); and Stock paraphrases a letter
from Pound to a Japanese friend in 1940, saying that
there had been some civilization in the United States
until 1863 (p. 495). Pound didn't say why he chose that
year rather than any other, but three obvious reasons
suggest themselves: (1) on January 1, 1863, Lincoln
issued the Emancipation Proclamation; (2) on July 4,
1863, with Grant's capture of Vicksburg, the Union
began to win the Civil War; and (3) the day before, with
Lee's defeat at Gettysburg, the Confederacy had lost its
last chance to win: as Winston Churchill said, "The

South had shot its bolt" (*A History of the English Speaking Peoples,* IV, 241). Pound indicated his own attitude toward that war in a propaganda broadcast from Rome on March 15, 1942, by quoting with approval Rudyard Kipling's statement about it: "The Americans obligingly slaughtered each other in order that the Czecho-Slovaks might inherit Boston Common" (Chace, p. 230). George Orwell, who thought it was ridiculous to accuse the political simpleton P. G. Wodehouse of treason because of his childish wartime broadcasts for the Nazis, took a much more serious view of Pound's for Mussolini: "His broadcasts were disgusting. I remember at least one in which he approved the massacre of the East European Jews and 'warned' the American Jews that their turn was coming presently" (*Collected Essays,* etc., IV, 490; cf. II, 183, 206; III, 84–85).

So much for the political and social notions that underlay Pound's poetry and criticism. These few representative samples must do.

Why did he give himself to such notions rather than to ideas worthy of his powers? The leaning toward rightist authoritarianism in politics seems to have resulted from tendencies or predilections of a more intimate, personal, pre-political kind. Pound's never-failing sense that he was an outsider caused him to play the role throughout his life in two radically different theatrical modes—often simultaneously, with resultant discords and incoherencies.

On the one hand he was attracted to the *noh* plays (which really should be called *yes* plays), those stylized ritual celebrations of the aristocratic virtues of obedience, respect and reverence toward those above oneself in the divinely ordained hereditary hierarchy, indifference or at most contempt toward those below oneself, and—regardless of one's position—readiness to die for the sake of the hierarchy, without which one's existence would be inconceivable. On the other hand, feeling himself an alien in a world where the principle of hereditary hierarchy was officially disavowed, he played throughout his life the ineluctably servile role of impudent entertainer.

That role has perhaps never been so richly developed as in the *commedia dell'arte,* a rowdy Renaissance genre in which the actors, representing stock characters and working from an outline of a situation, improvised the dialogue and action. Pound usually performed either as the Learned Doctor (a pedant from the University of Bologna, who made a career of displaying his learning to the ignorant, speaking to them in a hoity-toity accent that was supposed to be pure Bologna, and throwing in Latin, Greek and nonsense words), or as one or the other of the two Zanies, Brighella the intriguer (an analogue of Till Eulenspiegel and an ancestor of Rameau's nephew) and Harlequin the coarse and stupid buffoon: e.g., Pound's characteristic description of *Guide to Kulchur,* in a letter to E. V. Morley of Faber & Faber, as "Wot Ez knows, all of it, fer 7 and sax pence. . . . a bukk about Kulchur" (Stock, p. 442). Pound seems also to have fancied himself in two Biblical roles: the prophet, who is not without honor except in his own country, and Wisdom, who crieth in the streets and is not regarded. (See Pierre Louis Duchartre, *The Italian Comedy,* trans. Randolph T. Weaver [London: Harrap, 1929; rpt. Dover, 1966], pp. 123–78, 196–207.)

But if this were the whole truth about Pound he would not be worth considering. We consider him because in addition to being a fool and an evil mountebank of the type of Thomas Mann's Cipolla, he was a great man. His generosity—with his time, his influence, his money to the extent that he had it, and other people's money to the extent that he could get at it—was as unlimited as his hatred and vulgarity. And, equally to the point, his artistic judgment was usually of the best. He helped Joyce. He helped Eliot. He helped Marianne Moore. He helped William Carlos Williams.

He helped E. E. Cummings. He helped Robert Frost. He helped H.D., quite independently of the fact that he had once loved her. He helped Jacob Epstein, Jew though he was, recognizing good sculpture when he saw it. He helped Louis Zukofsky, Jew though he was, overestimating his talent to the extent of calling him "the only intelligent man in America" (Stock, p. 390). He resurrected Vivaldi long before the current revival—in 1936. He persuaded James Laughlin to start New Directions. He was good for literature; to the extent that the other arts interested him, he was good for them. If we accept Sainte-Beuve's dictum that *the* test of a critic is his judgment of his contemporaries—and it doesn't matter that Sainte-Beuve flunked his own test—Pound was perhaps the best critic of the twentieth century; moreover, he acted on his critical appreciations in practical ways—raising money, introducing people, etc. But for him we might very well not have *Ulysses;* but for him we most probably would not have *The Waste Land—* we almost certainly would not have it as it is, purged of all ordinariness. To the man who was so largely responsible for our having the best poem in English of the twentieth century, and the second-best novel ever written in English (*Finnegans Wake* being the first-best), we must be grateful, however much we despise his non-artistic judgments and the words and acts in which he expressed them.

His lament in old age, "Everything I touch, I destroy. I have always blundered" (Chace, p. xiii, note 1), was too categorical; his economic salvation-shouting and his snarling hatred of the democracy that regards neither race nor cult, in the event, did not demonstrably damage any particular person but himself. It is hardly conceivable that he converted to racism or anti-Semitism anyone who was not already so inclined. Nevertheless, inasmuch as he demonstrably contributed to the ambience of prejudice in which we live, he damaged us all: not only us who are objects of prejudice but also those who, like himself, have their vision blurred and distorted by it; those who waver; and those who with unwavering good will are distressed.

But his literary influence has been largely good. He was and is the teacher of every writer who cares to learn. In December 1958 Babette Deutsch suggested that all poets could learn a great deal from his emendations of *The Waste Land* if they were available (*Yale Literary Magazine,* quoted in *A Casebook on Ezra Pound,* ed. William Van O'Connor and Edward Stone [New York: Thomas Y. Crowell, 1959], pp. 151–52). Now that they are available, it is clear that she was right. Even we who write mere expository prose can learn a great deal from them; and as teachers, if we could ever in this lapsed age get past the necessity of correcting mere incoherencies, grammatical errors, misspellings, inaccuracies of vocabulary, etc., we could use Valerie Eliot's facsimile edition as an excellent textbook of writing. It is a practical application of the principles Pound was to state systematically in *ABC of Reading* (New York: New Directions, 1934), which would also be a useful textbook if students were technically able to follow its advice. (But there's no point in trying to teach figure skating to people who can't stay on their feet.)

I am not a Pound specialist, and I have not read all or even most of his criticism; but almost everything that I have read has been pure gold. He made mistakes now and then: he thought Wyndham Lewis was a better novelist than Joyce; he thought Joyce was only doing better what Flaubert had already done well; the "Sirens" chapter of *Ulysses* first bewildered and then shocked him; *Finnegans Wake* was beyond him; Milton was beyond him, for political reasons; he said Proust merely followed in the wake of James; it seems to me that he overestimated Landor's verse, perhaps in sympathy for his acidulous striving with almost everybody; and in at least one case Pound was guilty of an error of fact with regard to literature: he said that Gavin Douglas's translation of the

Aeneid was "better than the original, as Douglas had heard the sea" ("How to Read," in *Literary Essays of Ezra Pound,* ed. T. S. Eliot [New York: New Directions Paperbook, 1968], p. 35; and cf. *ABC of Reading,* p. 118). Vergil had heard the sea, having lived at Naples and Brindisi. Even granting for the sake of argument that the translation is better than the original, and ignoring the fact that Vergil had heard the sea, the argument is a non sequitur. But there aren't many such weak spots in Pound's criticism. Most of it that I have read is uncommonly refreshing. I can still read with joy almost everything in *Literary Essays, ABC of Reading, The Spirit of Romance,* Forrest Read's useful gathering *Pound/Joyce,* and the literary parts of *Guide to Kulchur* (to the extent that I can read them, having little Greek and no Chinese).

Pound's poetry has always seemed to me his least valuable literary work. I think that Eliot was not insincere but finely ambiguous in calling him "il miglior fabbro," for that is the title of a chapter in *The Spirit of Romance* dealing with Arnaut Daniel, and Pound at his best as a poet was often an imitator of Arnaut, Bertran de Born and other poets east and west who had the qualities he most prized: the singing line, the clear image, the natural figure, the one right word. He himself achieved these qualities over and over again, but always in an obviously mannered way: for—his denials notwithstanding—he was an aesthete, an antiquarian, a pasticheur, a bookish poet. His translations of romance lyric poems are highly successful, carrying over both the prose sense and the lyricism; but his own lyric poems often read like highly successful translations. The beginning of Canto XXX, Nietzscheism in antique costume, is a fine example: "Compleynt, compleynt I hearde upon a day, ..." His literary nature was largely second nature. He said, "Make it new," but when he was at his best he made it old: even his most intensely personal utterances tended to be in antique diction: "Pull down thy vanity, I say pull down" (Canto LXXXI).

His bookishness is also one of the causes of the incoherence that afflicts the Cantos, an incoherence he admitted and regretted (Stock, p. 590). Canto LII, for example, contains (in no necessary order) allusions to and images of Italy, Spain, Germany, Greece, China, Sligo and London, quotations from Hjalmar Schacht, John Adams and Lord Palmerston, a spurious line that professional anti-Semites attribute to Benjamin Franklin, and throughout the last two-thirds an imitation of Hesiod's *Works and Days* in Chinese terms. Even this passage, which stays with one subject to the unusual length of three pages, lacks Hesiod's unity, coherence and emphasis, for, unlike the *Works and Days,* it is drawn from books, not from personal experience. It is factitious. It is second-hand.

Bookishness is not necessarily a weakness, unless you are prepared, as I am not, to consider every literary and allusive poem inferior to every poem that doesn't depend on our having read anything else. The essential weakness of all of Pound's poetry is not its artificiality but its intellectual invalidity—and I use the word "invalidity" in its strict sense: lack of internal consistency. I think most readers would agree with me that one of the best of his poems is Canto XLV, "With Usura." It has to a wonderfully high degree all the qualities he most prized, in the idiom he most successfully affected; part of its appeal, accordingly, is the appeal of the antique, of *musica antiqua;* it is an indoor, delicate, bookish poem; it makes fine use of books on technique, poetics, craft, and it uses them in the service of his unteachable gift that came not from books but from God. God is not an intellectual, however, and the intellectual content of "With Usura" is—not nil, but false: a minus quantity. Minus? Minus.

Many good poems have no intellectual content— "Come unto these yellow sands," for example, and "In a Station of the Métro"—but they don't claim any and don't need any. "With Usura" does claim valid intellectual content; of its total claim as a poem, therefore, part is invalid, and the whole suffers from that invalidity. Pound believed that the government should own the banks and lend tax money for capital purposes without interest; by implication, avoiding modern examples, he applied the medieval term "usura," with all its connotations of high risk and high interest and officially condoned illegality and immorality, to the limited risks and limited interest rates of modern banks. In the first place, to do so is to misuse the term "usura"; in the second place, the insinuation that the modern credit system is destructive is simply false, as anybody knows who has ever built a house with a bank loan; in the third place, even if modern banks were engaged in usury, since Pound admired medieval and Renaissance brigandage without reservation he was not on moral ground so high that he could look down on other methods of enriching oneself at the expense of others. These arguments of course have nothing to do with poetry, but neither has the argument of the poem; being a false argument, it damages the poem.

The modern version, "With usury has no man a good house," in Canto LI, is much inferior, though the prose message is the same. (Pound needed a friend to do for him what he did for Eliot.) The superiority of "With Usura" is not intellectual but poetic, a matter not of ideas but of technique —in poetry, Pound was seldom quite at home with modern English—but both versions would be better if they expressed a valid idea. Longinus—or whoever wrote *On the Sublime*—said it some time ago.

From time to time Pound said that of course not all banks were owned by Jews and not all Jews were usurers (Stock, pp. 478–79, 508–9). At least once he said he didn't recommend genocide: "Don't start a pogrom, that is, not an old style killing of small Jews. That system is no good, whatever. Of course, if some man had a stroke of genius, and could start a pogrom up at the top . . . there might be something to say for it. But on the whole, legal measures are preferable" (Stock, p. 508).

On the whole. Such statements, unsatisfactory as they are, were mere eddies on the edges of the rushing muddy torrent of his madness. The charge of usury was merely an effort to rationalize the irrational fury with which he hated Jews *as Jews;* since this absolute hatred involved an absolute denial of observable facts that he sometimes recognized, whenever he made it the intellectual content of his poetry it damaged his poetry *as poetry.* Canto XXXV, for example—"So this is (may we take it) Mitteleuropa:"—is as cheap as anything by Gerald L. K. Smith or Pound's collaborator John Kasper, executive secretary of the Seaboard White Citizens Councils and publisher of the secessionist *Clinton–Knox County Stars and Bars* (Stock, p. 556). A schlock emotion cannot be expressed except in schlock terms; they make Canto XXXV a schlock poem. The element of schlock damages the Cantos pretty much throughout. There are many lines and passages of great beauty, but they are thickly interspersed with lines and passages of the most contemptible cheapness: cheapness of language, of thought, of feeling. The tragedy of Ezra Pound was the tragedy of a man who combined with an exquisite talent an often uncontrollable need to conduct revahval meetns. A writer's utterance is his soul; and what is he profited, as a writer, if he shall save the whole world and damage his own utterance?[5]

[5] After writing this chapter, I began to feel guilty about not having read Hugh Kenner's *The Pound Era* (Berkeley: University of California Press, 1971). Now, having read it, I admit that I had formed an ill opinion of it beforehand, anticipating that it would reflect the same yearning back toward pre-democratic hierarchy and pre-scientific dogmatism that vitiated *The Stoic Comedians* and *Dublin's Joyce.* As indeed it does. Among other disingenuousnesses, Kenner denies that Pound knew that the Nazis wanted to exterminate the Jews; he denies that most Germans knew; he says that Pound's anti-Semitic scurrilities in Canto LII are "part of a diagnosis . . . tending rather to decrease than to encourage anti-Semitism" (p. 465); he says Pound's scurrilous wartime broadcasts misrepresented his true intentions because they were inadvertently delivered through "the persona of a folk Isaiah" (p. 468); he seems not to know that everything valid C. H. Douglas said

I. The Merchant of Venice   It seems likely that Dickens catered to the anti-Semitism of his time without having given much thought to it. It is not possible to suppose any such thing of Shakespeare. In *The Merchant of Venice,* clearly, he catered to anti-Semitism knowing full well what it was, how it operated, and what practical effects it had.

Chapter 10
Prejudice and
Literature

Elizabethan-Jacobean society, to be sure, was not that of a twentieth-century liberal democracy. It was a society in which Ben Jonson's appallingly cheap *Irish Masque* amused the court; in which a gentleman of the court, Edmund Spenser, could seriously and without any sense of impropriety recommend that the Irish be exterminated; in which Jews were not legally permitted to live; and in which a converted Jew from Portugal, Dr. Roderigo Lopez, the Queen's physician, could be convicted of having conspired to poison her, at a trial in which the Earl of Essex was (1) the chief political plotter and accuser, (2) the prosecuting attorney, with the rack at his disposal, and (3) the judge. (See John Palmer, *Political and Comic Characters of Shakespeare* [New York: Macmillan, 1962], pp. 401–4.)

But even so. *Shakespeare!*

He was not thoughtlessly committed to the conventional attitudes of his time and place; he did not automatically blend, with the chameleon automatism of a

about the abuses of monopoly capitalism had already been said by Thorstein Veblen, whose *The Theory of Business Enterprise* (1903) had predicted the coming of fascism not as a cure but as an exacerbation of the disease; and he shares Pound's romantic ignorance of the cheap conscripted labor that built cathedrals. But, like Pound himself, *The Pound Era* is too complex to be merely scorned. It is a work of wide-ranging scholarship, combining the methods of Boswell, Francis Parkman and John Livingston Lowes; it is full of analogous discoveries; its readings of Pound's poetry are extraordinarily sensitive and enlightening; it has persuaded me of the greatness, however shamefully disfigured, of the Cantos; but the best parts are the digressions on Eliot and Williams.

thoughtless man, into the local color or into what
Larbaud would have called the temporal color. He did
dare to take thought. He affords no comfort to
relativists, historicists, careerists, opportunists or
ass-kissers. But the fact is that he did quite deliberately
write an anti-Semitic play.

In 1594 Dr. Lopez was convicted and hanged, drawn
and quartered; Christopher Marlowe's *The Jew of Malta,*
which had first been acted several years before (the
estimates vary from 1588 to 1592), was immediately
revived to cash in on the wave of anti-Semitism, and
had a great success; Shakespeare wrote *The Merchant
of Venice* in 1594–95, while Marlowe's play was still
running, and it was produced in 1596–97, also with great
success.

It seems to have been put together or pieced together
under the constraint of a troubling occasion. I say this
because it is one of Shakespeare's shorter plays, and it
would be considerably shorter without three thick wads
of padding: the test of the caskets (I.ii, II.i, II.ix and
III.ii), the by-play of Launcelot Gobbo and his father
(II.ii), and the whole of Act V, a long anti-climactic
extension. Shakespeare seems for once not to have
known quite how to handle his assignment. For he was
required, for once, to do something cheap.

Inherently cheap. *The Merchant of Venice* is cheap in the
same way that *The Birth of a Nation* is cheap, and for the
same reason: not even the greatest master of technique
can make a valid work of art if he has to appeal, or
chooses to appeal, to a phony emotion. The prejudicial
emotions, being not spontaneous but induced, not
personal but imitated, are as phony as hit-parade love or
recruiting-poster patriotism or amusement-arcade
pleasure. There is no nature in them; they are hard-sold
and soft-sold with malice aforethought. In Shakespeare's
England, where there were few or no Jews, there was
nevertheless widespread anti-Semitism, even before the
Lopez affair—as the popularity of *The Jew of Malta*
indicated. Was that hatred of an abstraction a natural

emotion? It was on a par with my schoolmates' contempt for dagoes.

I suggest that Shakespeare found the assignment awkward: that he saw through the preconceptions he catered to. Why else would the play be so disconnected in its construction and so inconsistent in its psychology? Portia is pieced together as arbitrarily as the play is pieced together.

In the first performances Shylock was evidently played for laughs. T. W. Baldwin's charts in *The Organization and Personnel of the Shakespearean Company* (Princeton: Princeton University Press, 1927; rpt. Russell and Russell, 1961) show that the role was played by Thomas Pope, the chief comic, whose other roles were Jaques in *As You Like It,* Sir Toby Belch in *Twelfth Night,* Buckingham in *Richard III,* Quince in *A Midsummer Night's Dream,* Petruchio in *The Taming of the Shrew,* Philip Faulconbridge in *King John,* Mowbray in *Richard II,* Falstaff in *Henry IV* 1 and 2, Armado in *Love's Labour's Lost,* Mercutio in *Romeo and Juliet,* Benedick in *Much Ado About Nothing,* Fluellen in *Henry V,* Casca in *Julius Caesar,* Parolles in *All's Well that Ends Well,* Dromio of Syracuse in *The Comedy of Errors,* Speed in *Two Gentlemen of Verona,* York in *Henry VI* 1, 2 and 3, Aaron in *Titus Andronicus,* and the First Player in *Hamlet.* With three exceptions, these were comic parts, high or middle or low; and the exceptions were a hypocrite (Buckingham), a roarer (Mowbray), and a devilish villain (Aaron). Thus, neither before nor after playing Shylock did Pope ever play a character of tragic dignity; thus, if Shylock was conceived as a character of tragic dignity he was egregiously miscast in the production that Shakespeare had a hand in.

He was not so conceived. He has no dignity at all. In his literary descent he is a half-brother of Antonio, both being descended on one side from the *commedia dell'arte*'s Venetian Merchant, nicknamed Pantaloon (Duchartre, pp. 179–95). In some scenarios Pantaloon is rich, in others poor, but in none has he any dignity whatever. When he is rich he keeps running down to the harbor to see if his ships full of merchandise have come in—but they don't come in, and he is ruined and everybody laughs at his loud ridiculous anguish; or he spends his time gloating over a hoard of ducats and jewels in his cellar—but he is defrauded of them by a rival, or by his wife (who also cuckolds him), or by his daughter (who has an affair under his nose), or by his female servants (who abet the daughter's or the wife's naughtiness), or by his valet (whom he starves—in fact, he starves everybody in the house except himself); or he has retired from business and spends his time chasing women, who either rebuff him or exploit him, or meddling in the affairs of his neighbors, who ridicule him and make him the butt of practical jokes. When he is poor he devotes himself to rebuilding his fortune, but everyone mocks his ridiculously desperate efforts and little boys follow him through the streets jeering.

But though Antonio and Shylock are thus literary half-brothers, there is little resemblance between them. Antonio is repeatedly praised in his absence (II.viii.35–49, III.i.12–13, III.ii. 292–96);[6] but Shylock is repeatedly referred to as a devil (II.ii.20–29, III.i.18–19, III.i.68–69); "Our house is hell," says Jessica (II.iii.2), and it is intimated, both behind his back and to his face, that he is not really the father of the "gentle" Jessica (II.iii.11–12, III.i.34–36, III.v.5–16), gentle because gentile because gentle because . . . (II.iv.19, 24, II.vi.51, and in the last line of the Duke's sarcastic speech at the trial, IV.i.34). Everyone mocks, insults and abuses Shylock, assuming as a matter of course that that is the proper way to treat a Jew. Antonio, the one seemingly honest person in this totally cynical play, the only one

---

[6] The line numbers refer to lines in the 1970 revised edition of the Pelican Shakespeare paperback.

who never plays with outward deceits and false appearances, is even ruder than the others in his treatment of Shylock. It seems to me fairly obvious that Shakespeare must have read Sartre's *Anti-Semite and Jew*, for Antonio in this regard conforms exactly to Sartre's "Portrait of the Anti-Semite." I seem to have lent it to somebody, so I can't quote it; but the essential point is that the anti-Semite chooses to be irrational because the armor of irrationality is impenetrable and makes him superior to facts, to rational statements, and to expectations of decent behavior. Thus it guarantees him victory without argument. He doesn't argue. He makes an outrageously irrational statement; you counter it with a fact or a syllogism; he listens, smiling or frowning, until you stop speaking, and then makes another outrageously irrational statement, or simply repeats the first. Since he scorns facts and reasons, he doesn't bother to present his position seriously; since he doesn't respect you, he doesn't care whether you respect him or not; he destroys the basis of rational discourse by refusing to engage in it, even within himself; there is no possible way for a rational person to deal with him; he is proof against logic, language, evidence, taste, personal honor, and even the conventions of normal human communication, chief of which is a willingness to communicate. Willingness to communicate, to argue, involves the unspoken assumption that there is some purpose in communicating and arguing—i.e., that the truth is not already plain beyond argument—and the further assumption that your interlocutor is human. Willingness to argue is a liberal trait.

Antonio, in his behavior toward Shylock, is illiberal and irrational. To Shylock's outraged statement that Antonio should not try to borrow money from a man he has spat on, kicked, and called dog, he replies,

> I am as like to call thee so again,
> To spit on thee again, to spurn thee too.
> [I.ii.125–26.]

This speech undoubtedly won approval and perhaps applause from Shakespeare's audience, who found in it a wish-fulfillment. Any defiant or contemptuous speech by a hero to a villain arouses enthusiasm in those who identify with the hero: it affords them the cheap non-literary pleasure of a daydream—a vicarious experience they can enjoy without the exertion of will and courage involved in a real act of defiance or contempt.

This vicarious experience—this cheap thrill—is especially cheap when the hero's superiority to the villain is not a real but a merely conventional superiority, the assumed superiority of one ethnic group to another. All the Christian characters in the play—even Launcelot Gobbo and Lorenzo—are assumed to have this superiority; and Antonio, in addition, is repeatedly asserted to have a real, personal superiority. Thus, in the eyes of Shakespeare's audience, he is doubly superior to Shylock. Therefore it is right and proper that there should be sympathy for Antonio's potential losses (I.i.15–39, in which Solanio and Salerio talk the way Pantaloon acts), but only mockery for Shylock's actual losses (II.viii.12–24).

Shylock's two defiant speeches—"Signior Antonio, many a time and oft" (I.iii.102–24) and "To bait fish withal" (III.i.46–64)—explain but do not justify his evil behavior. Such speeches are a familiar feature in Shakespeare's presentation of his villains. Shylock's lifetime of being insulted is analogous to Richard III's physical deformity and Edmund Gloucester's bastardy. Like theirs, his speeches attempting to justify his behavior don't justify it at all. However much we may sympathize with them, we cannot accept their cruelty.

In Shylock's case, moreover, the speeches cannot have aroused the sympathy of Shakespeare's audience—and, Shakespeare being a highly competent technician, we may doubt that they were intended to. Since they came from the mouth of a devilish stage Jew represented by a well-known comic wearing a red wig, the audience must

have found them hilarious—as it would have found
hilarious a speech full of outraged dignity in the mouth
of Caliban. My wife says the language of the speeches
seems to indicate understanding and respect on
Shakespeare's part. She suggests that perhaps
Shakespeare wanted to raise questions in the minds of
the audience but found it inadvisable to raise them for
more than a moment, and that in any case a good comic
actor could keep the speeches in character. I fully agree.
I suggest that Pope—doubtless with Shakespeare's
approval—delivered them in the manner of the *commedia
dell'arte:* with facial contortions, vocal contortions, and
exaggerated pantomimic writhing and gesturing of the
whole body: "Hath not a Jew HANDS?"

This view of the *way* the speeches were delivered
reduces the difficulty they present to readers. Just as the
King could do no wrong, even if he did, so Shylock
could not do or say anything dignified, even if he did.
Like his ancestor Pantaloon, he was a comic butt to be
abused as a matter of course, no matter what he might
say or do. His function was to serve as an outlet for
sadistic tendencies. The sexual element was provided by
the torturer, a woman dressed as a man. During the trial
scene the audience undoubtedly experienced a delicious
release of sadism, directed first (with a thrill of horror
and much misgiving) against Antonio, then triumphantly
redirected against Shylock. In periods of feverishly
intense racial or religious prejudice, all society (with a
few embarrassed but impotent exceptions) becomes a
mob. Thus Shakespeare's audience (in which pretty
much all classes were represented), having been titillated
with the uneasy prospect of gratifying unlicensed sadism
at the expense of a prosperous member of society—a
real human sacrifice—was reprieved at the last moment
and given a more acceptable thrill through the provision
of a safe victim—a devil in human form, who had just
tried to sell the idea that he was really human, but who
if you pricked him would not bleed—an outsider against
whom sadism was licensed. That is one of the classic

social functions of the Jews and other "inferior races," lesser breeds without the law. We afford opportunities for lawless behavior within the law. We divert the mob. That is the meaning of Bebel's remark, "Anti-Semitism is the socialism of fools."[7]

Shakespeare seems to have been influenced by Bebel as much as by Sartre. Even if he didn't share his audience's vulgar delusion, in catering to it he wrote a vulgar play. Of course the play works in the theater. But so does *The Birth of a Nation*, whose vulgarity I think no reader who has got this far will deny. And directors who present *The Merchant of Venice* as a tragedy, with Shylock as the hero, add to the vulgarity of the original conception the vulgarity of misinterpretation, making the play even less valid.

II. THE TAMING OF THE SHREW   The trouble with prejudices is that if they aren't challenged we don't recognize them as prejudices; and the more widespread they are, the less liable they are to be challenged. In Shakespeare's day neither Jews nor women had any public voice; the popular beliefs as to what they were and how they should be treated were never challenged; and Shakespeare, as the most popular playwright, both accepted and reinforced the popular beliefs.

The Taming of the Shrew (1594) was one of a number of plays dramatizing the right and proper subordination of women to men: *The Four P's* (1569), *The Patient Grissil* (1598), *A Woman Killed with Kindness* (1603), and *Rule a Wife and Have a Wife* (1624). As these dates indicate, there was no steady or persistent demand for such plays, as if the point needed to be proved; the assumption underlying them all was taken for granted.

At the beginning of *The Taming of the Shrew*, Katherine

For a few modern instances of lawlessness within the law, see the story "Alabama Official Expects to Find 1963 Killers of Four Black Girls," *The New York Times*, Wednesday, March 10, 1976, p. 14. The quoted editorial comment of *The Alabama Journal* is especially pertinent.

is continually in a rage, struggling to break out of a world in which men make all the decisions and women are forced to give their hands against their hearts, being no more than goods and chattels—i.e., cattle; but there is no other world. At the end of the play she has armed herself with the useless weapon of the unarmed, irony: her excessive obedience is a mockery of her husband's values and his world, but it has no effect, because—well, there are two possibilities. Either he is unaware of being mocked, or he is aware and amused.

If he is unaware, it is because he is encased in the impenetrable armor of a vulgarity incapable of conceiving that the conventions it lives by are not self-evident truths, or that they can be mocked by exaggerated acquiescence. This is the insensitivity of Achilles numbed by the river of death except where his mother's hand has touched him—and let us recall that only a god or a sexy woman could find that spot.

But a male chauvinist, like an anti-Semite, may deliberately disregard what his conscious mind tells him. If this is Petruchio's position, then Katherine is in the position described by Stephen Dedalus as that of a jester, "indulged and disesteemed, winning a clement master's praise" (James Joyce, *Ulysses* [Modern Library, 1961 ed.], 25.9–10).

In either case, Katherine is as abnormal at the end of the play as at the beginning—just as much an object of wonder to all who see her. She has, to be sure, gained the amusement of being a spectator of the farce in which she is a victim; to this extent she escapes into a world of her own—but, like all private worlds, it is a delusion.

Not a complete delusion, however. She has not done to herself what the unnamed Lord of the Induction has done to Christopher Sly. She knows that what has changed is not the situation but only her view of it. Having substituted irony for violence, she is more bitter at the end of the play than at the beginning. In any case, and whatever the case may be, her husband doesn't care.

Nor, apparently, does Shakespeare. In *The Taming of the Shrew*, as in *The Merchant of Venice*, he has catered to gross vulgarity and been grossly vulgar.

Let us not be overawed, even by Shakespeare, so far that we can't recognize vulgarity for what it is when it solicits our participation like a whore on a street corner.

Does that partly answer your question?